Sergeant:
My 34 Years Behind the Badge

by Detective Sergeant Mickey Chernetsky (Retired)

PublishAmerica
Baltimore

First printing

Hardcover 978-1-4489-2571-1
Softcover 1-60474-034-5
PAperback 978-1-4512-7099-0
PUBLISHED BY PUBLISHAMERICA, LLLP
www.publishamerica.com
Baltimore

Printed in the United States of America

Introduction

Do you know what cops do? They respond to calls for help on a daily basis. They do their job to guarantee that we live in a safe society. Some officers have been killed in the line of duty while in the performance of their job.

In this book I call *Sergeant*, I will attempt to give you a walk on the inside of a cop's mind. These are just short glimpses into people's lives, as police officers jump from one call to another during their eight-hour tour of duty.

I became one of those officers when I joined the Buffalo, New York, Police Department on July 31, 1961, working the job both as a patrolman and later as an investigator, reaching the rank of detective sergeant. I put 34 years on this job while walking this thin blue line.

Some police officers have
more stories,
some have less,
some are more heroic,
some are less,

than mine. But I wanted to share with you my experiences about my life as a police officer!

As an investigator, I picked up the pieces of various lives along the way. I might have been fortunate enough to satisfy them, but other times I was not.

One thing is certain though, the stories and events are always there.

Whether you are a police officer, a firefighter, or a rescue worker, no one can take away the frustrations that they undergo as they deal with the ordeals confronting them on a daily basis. These feelings sometimes stay with you your whole life.

Mainly because
of what you have seen,

or what you have heard,
or what you have smelled,
or what you have touched.

It is always locked away in your consciousness and there is no escape from it. Some police officers can only talk to each other about what is inside their heads, while going to cop bars after work because they can't take this job home with them.

Did you know that recent data indicates that law enforcement officers have the highest suicide rate, divorce rate, and alcoholism rate, among other professions?

Some officers crumble under the stress and do not survive, by taking their own life. Unfortunately, I knew a few officers who have committed suicide while on the job, for whatever reason caused them to take such drastic action. I have written this subject in a separate chapter on police suicides.

So walk with me, while I tell you what cops do, live, and sometimes die in their chosen profession behind this Thin Blue Line! I have chosen to list these stories in alphabetical order relative to their chapter titles.

Chapter One
Accidents

Thinking back, it had been an eventful year so far and I looked forward to my first assignment, after going through the death of my father in April, going on the police department in July, and getting married in September.

* * *

The police car is the first line of defense! It begins the officer's day! There you are, inside this capsule, with your siren, lights, computer, uniform, gun, etc, and you sit there awaiting the day, wondering what lies ahead. You leap to the sound of the radio dispatcher. You feel that you are invincible, like in an armored battle tank! You are in a marked black-and-white with the word "police" all over it! You're going to take on the world! But are you that secure in your protective bubble? The following are stories about what happened to me on several occasions while in this supposed safe environment. The first accident is in a marked vehicle.

It Came out of Nowhere

My mind flashes back to when I was a rookie. After I finished the police academy, my first assignment was in September of 1961 at Precinct #15, located in the South Buffalo section of Buffalo, New York.

We were on patrol in our sector of the precinct. An Irish cop by the name of Richard was the driver. He was five years older than me, five feet ten inches tall, of heavy build, round faced, and had dark hair. [1] (*I was 25 years of age!*)

It was in the middle of summer, on a dark night. All was quite on the street.

We were engaged in a conversation about our families, when all of a sudden the stillness ended, when Bang!

We were hit as a car crashed into us from behind. We felt the impact as our heads went forward and then backward, the result of which ended with both of us in the hospital, after being jerked in our seats. However our injuries were not serious.

A description was written up in the local newspaper about this accident which stated: "Two police officers from the South Park station obtained injuries in a car accident, when a driver, caused a three-car accident, and hit their patrol car from behind." We were not that safe after all, because the car that hit our police cruiser from behind had faulty brakes!

* * *

In another accident some years later, while riding in an unmarked vehicle, I was on an elite squad, known as the robbery squad. It was dusk, and a light rain was falling. "Officer in trouble," the radio blared! My partner, Joe, was behind the wheel. Joe is six feet five inches tall, weighs 280 pounds, bald, with a full round face and blue eyes. He always had a large cigar in his mouth which would annoy the chief of detectives because it distorted his TV image when we appeared on TV while in the investigation of street crimes.[2]

"Let's go," Joe screamed, as he hit the siren and flashing light button to respond to this urgent call. We were speeding to the scene as this is a call all officers respond to. *It could be me, calling for help,* goes through their minds. We weaved through traffic, at about 50 MPH, as this is a good speed to get anywhere in the city safely. But we were soon to find out we were not safe, as we were hit broadside by a taxi that ran a red light.

The point of impact was slightly to the rear of the driver's door. If we had been hit at a different angle, it would have surely killed Joe. Our vehicle spun around in the street and then slammed into a telegraph pole on the opposite side of the street.

A siren wailed in the distance
The sound came closer
Closer

And the wail stopped as it reached its destination. It was us!

Our ambulance arrived on the scene! At that time I felt someone fumbling around my belt trying to steal my weapon from my holster. I clamped my arm against my side as I struggled to hold on to my revolver. He didn't succeed! And then I was loaded into the ambulance. There was no more silence, as the wail of the siren screamed again, as we raced to a nearby hospital. Joe received shoulder, rib, and ankle injuries, while I received arm, hip, and head injuries. I'll repeat, everyone answers this type of call, thinking, *It could be me calling for help!*

* * *

In yet another mishap, I was saved by an unusual manner. You would think that a vest was supposed to save you from being shot and stop a bullet's impact. Listen to this story of an accident report. I have to say that my vest saved me not from bullets but from the crash!

We were in a high-crime-rate area of the city. The driver was a detective named Pat. He was tall, slim build, with combed-back straight hair.

We were struck

All of a sudden a car came out of nowhere and struck my side of the car and into my door panel. I could feel the collision as it hit us! I felt a pain in my side. Again, I was loaded into an ambulance and taken to the hospital. The doctor who treated me said, "If it wasn't for your bulletproof vest, you would have had cracked ribs." I was lucky that I had it on as it absorbed the shock at my rib cage.

Accidents in police vehicles do happen as indicated in the above stories, when officers end up in the hospital while they are on patrol answering calls.

So you are not more immune while in a police car than in any other car after all!

Nor are you safe while investigating some crimes which are not related to your specialty, as you will see in the following chapter on arson.

Chapter Two
Arson

Arson was not our job but sometimes you find yourself ending up being involved anyway as indicated in the following stories. Let me tell you about three incidents which happened to me, which touched the crime of arson.

In the first incident, we were listening to testimony in an arson case in the courtroom when we heard shots

The courtroom was jammed with spectators, when all of a sudden

Pow!

Pow!

A man in the spectator section had pulled out a gun, and fired at a witness who was on the stand.

The judge had to dive for cover under a desk. Before we could react, the officer of the court quickly went into action. He was alongside the gunman as he fired his weapon. This officer ended up with powder burns on his shirt as he disarmed the gunman. Thank God that no one was hit by the volley of shots.

The shooter was a victim himself, because he believed that the person who was testifying caused an arson in a house where his grandmother was seriously injured.

In the second incident, there was an arrest which I was involved in, while in a house that happened to go up in flames! Let me explain this episode to you. I was inside the house while undercover on the liquor squad. We were in the process of an arrest of two suspects in a suspected speakeasy. It was while we were in a violent struggle with these two men when other persons in the house ran out. I yelled to my partner, "I smell smoke, the house is on fire." Just then our backup came rushing up the stairs, and close behind them

14

were Buffalo firefighters, dragging their hoses. We learned later that the fire had been set by those who fled the house, thereby dousing the lower stairs with gasoline.

In the third incident, there was a situation when a store almost blew up while I was working a second job inside. The store had just undergone some major construction where they used propane heaters to dry some of the side walls and other areas.

I was summoned to the front of the store because of an arrest of a shoplifter. I couldn't believe my eyes! There was a person dousing a magazine rack with lighter fluid and then he took a cigarette lighter and set fire to it. He assumed everyone would rush to the fire and he would free his girlfriend who had been arrested.

My only thought was to get the fire out, so as to eliminate a risk of an explosion.

I was in plainclothes as I approached him, and caught him completely off guard. At the same time, while in a struggle with him, I pulled the magazines from the rack and stomped them out with my feet. He almost caused an explosion, because of the propane heaters in the store. I had to forcibly subdue him as I placed him under arrest.

Thank God, the fire was put out quickly before it had a chance to spread.

Remember this was on a second job I was working!

Being on the fringe of arsons still put us in danger. And speaking of danger, how would you feel if someone would try to kill you with a bomb! Read on!

Chapter Three
Bomb

Have you ever been confronted with the thought that you may be blown up? Well I have, and it was scary! I almost had a heart attack then.

Let me tell you about this unforeseen surprise I had waiting for me while at work in one of the hot precincts of the city. It all started with a routine fight on the street but the end was dramatic. Police cars responded to a disturbance on the street, and someone took a portable radio from their car while they were busy with this call.

The next day we questioned several of the local junkies, and told them that we wanted our radio back. "Just drop it off at the station house, and there would be no questions asked," we told them!

Yeah, They Dropped It Off All Right!

The very next day there were voices heard downstairs when the patrolmen returned to the station house. They noticed a package on one of the rear tables. Someone yelled up the stairs to me, "Special delivery for the sarge"

I was in the detectives' office when I heard, "Hey, Sarge, there's a package for you here, with your name on the outside." I was summoned to open it. I figured that this was our radio. I was shocked when I saw what it contained.

I said to everyone, "It looks like a bomb!" as there was a mad scrambling for the rear exit. But closer examination disclosed that it contained fake dynamite sticks, but with the original wrappings, along with a clock and some wires.

We notified the assistant chief of detectives, who said, "I'll send the bomb squad out there anyway. Don't you know that there could be resin in the wrappings, and it could still cause an explosion?" I was unaware that this could happen.

A member of the bomb squad came to the precinct and carefully examined the contents of the package while he probed it. He stood there with his body armor on, and then proclaimed, "It's safe, nothing to worry about."

"Great!" Everyone then breathed a sigh of relief. The panic was over, there was no explosion!

This event reminded some seasoned officers who recalled what happened in this precinct a year ago and they were afraid that this could have been a reoccurrence. At that time a real bomb was placed on the windowsill. Here's that account!

An officer went outside to catch a breath of fresh air.[3] He prevented a possible disaster, due to the fact that two individuals placed a real bomb on the windowsill near this same table area. There was a violent struggle as he fought with both men, and suffered stab wounds to his side and chest area. Even though wounded, he managed to get to his gun, and fired, thereby killing one of them as they attempted to escape.

And Later

Would you believe that this same officer had another altercation some months later? He was filmed by a camera crew who took pictures which showed him being stabbed by an assailant, when he went to the assistance of another detective, who was on the ground with a man who wielded a knife. "Shoot him! Shoot him!" yelled someone. But other officers were hesitant to shoot because they didn't want to hit of one of their own. This one particular officer managed to disarm him!

* * *

This was not my only experience with a bomb scare. There was a case in which we were looking for this individual who was a demolition expert.

It was one of the many times we were after this person we knew as "Frank." We had experiences with him on other occasions before this particular case even came about. He was a Vietnam veteran who had returned from the war with no skills other than demolition, guns, and combat training. He was in the habit of knocking off drug dealers and numbers game operators. A few of them he had killed in self-defense and got away with it, even though he went to trial on each one of them. They would find no cause to convict him.

This time, he thought he killed a man. Frank was wearing a ski mask at the time he committed this crime. This made him think that he was in the clear; however, he had made the fatal mistake of taking off his mask after he had shoved an ice pick into the victim's head. The ice pick went behind the victim's right ear, and the victim had taken a last glimpse of Frank before he went unconscious. He would be able to recognize him! A taxi driver found the victim staggering on the street with the ice pick broken off in his head. He was bleeding from numerous chest wounds, 13 to be exact, and there were also three wounds to his head. He identified Frank as the man who did this to him, and it was our job to serve the warrant on him, i.e. if we could find him because he was very elusive.

As I had indicated there were other times we had gone after him. He was always armed to the teeth, but he claimed that he had to be, as people wanted him dead. (*By armed, I meant legal guns, i.e. shotgun or rifle.*) In this recent search for him, we had received a tip and checked his previous address. We went up the stairs armed with carbines and shotguns. Then we saw it as someone yelled one word

"Wire! A wire in the doorframe!"

We all backed down the stairs in a hurry! A call to the bomb squad was made. Upon their arrival on the scene, they ended up finding a pipe bomb wired to the door, and figured that the suspect left in such haste that he did not have time to arm it. *We were lucky again!*

Frank would later call the police to turn himself in at Niagara Falls, a suburb outside of Buffalo. He wanted our lieutenant on the porch with him so we wouldn't shoot him. "I'm not afraid of anything, but I know that you guys are going to kill me," he told the lieutenant. We complied with his wishes, which resulted in his arrest. He served eight and one half years, instead of 25 years, for this assault on the victim of the ice pick attack. He didn't do the maximum time.

It wasn't over yet

I ran into him again, years later, after he got out of prison. On this particular encounter we answered a call of someone firing a machine gun into a liquor store. Upon our arrival on the scene, we could see bullet holes
in the liquor store windows,
in the car windows,
in the parking lot next door,
and in the windows of adjoining buildings.
Frank was the bodyguard for the owner of the liquor store, whose son had been killed in a gang shooting. Naturally, Frank didn't have a gun on him, but we knew that he had one hidden nearby. He looked at us and just smiled, and said, "I don't know who was shooting." But we knew that if one of them had entered the liquor store after their barrage of gunfire, he would have killed them.

You never know what might come your way on this job, as I did when I opened the package addressed to me, or when we spotted the wire in the doorframe. My body parts would have been scattered like the wind if there was an explosion!

Even while doing this dangerous job some officers have been able to educate themselves on a higher level for personal satisfaction. Follow along in the next chapter.

Chapter Four
College Life Again!

Some officers attend college while still on the job during their time off.

It was my intention to finish 20 years on the department and go into the teaching profession. I studied exceptional and elementary education while attending Buffalo State College in my off-duty time. *(I was also working another job at that time.)* The last block of teaching was full-time days, but I was unable to meet that requirement because my police schedule could not be adjusted at that time.

During this course I also did volunteer work with mentally retarded adults. However, I did manage to obtain a bachelor of arts in philosophy from the State University of New York College at Buffalo.

I had the opportunity to give lectures to officers at the Police Academy on bank robberies, and to utility companies on weapons and methods of the identification of holdup men. There was a photo taken which showed me and a secret service agent at a lecture to Niagara Mohawk employees, on holdup identification techniques and weapons used by holdup men.

So, you are making arrests during your career, but what happens when you are faced with the razzle-dazzle of our court system? See the next chapter!

Chapter Five
The Courts

The Door That Revolves

This is about the court system and what police officers have to put up with in regard to their testimony and the time they spend there. Let me start off by saying that I remember a phone call I received from a *New York Times* reporter who wanted my outlook on a rash of juvenile bank robberies which were occurring in Buffalo.

I told him, "The court system was nothing but a revolving door for criminals, in that, victims who wanted to see justice done will see the person who hurt them walk out the door again, almost at the same time they entered the door." The door that revolves

On this merry-go-round
that never stops spinning
Faster.
Victims and Criminals Round and round
Criminals and Victims Round and round
Faster,
Police and Judges Round and round
On this merry-go-round.

They didn't pay the police to go to court to testify, which forced law officers to go on their own time. Then they would adjourn the case, so that the officers had to come back, but at no cost to the city, but at a cost to the officers' families due to additional time spent away from them.

Some attorneys, not all, used to jerk the police around by waiting until a favorable judge was on the bench, or tell them the officer is not present, or just adjourn the case, which happened to me in the following story.

I made a statement in open court, in that I objected to this one particular series of adjournments. I told the judge, "My time is just as valuable as this attorney's." This was written in the next day's paper: "Is a detective's time as valuable as an attorney? Detective Chernetsky thinks so, and told the judge in open court." (*I didn't know that the press was there!*)

Questions Asked?

When you testify in the grand jury, some members sometimes ask you questions that would boggle your mind. I was asked by a lady who was seated in the jury box, "Isn't it true, Officer, that you are supposed to give them first shot, before you can shoot?"

Another jury member asked me, "Is your gun loaded?" because he heard that you cannot carry a loaded gun, and would only load it if you thought you had to use it.

Of course I responded saying, "That's not true," with a sincere look on my face, to both of the questions put to me.

The above question reminded me of a disagreement one religious officer had with his partner. He rode with this other detective, who happens to mention to him that he carries an unloaded gun. "I don't want to be in the situation to shoot someone," he said to his partner, who then replied, "I won't ride with you anymore unless you carry a loaded weapon."

He never thought that perhaps an individual might want to shoot him first, and that he would never be able to load his gun fast enough to properly defend himself. How is that for a scary event?

The door will keep spinning forever.

Were you ever caught in it and spit out?

What was your reaction to how you were treated or a member of your family was treated by this court system?

There are times when you are outside the realm of making arrests and have to put your life on the line by guarding someone as I explain in the following chapter concerning dignitaries.

Chapter Six
Dignitaries

We may rub elbows with persons who are dignitaries. Various officers are assigned to help out the Secret Service and our special service squad, whose duty it is to guard dignitaries who come to the city of Buffalo. Here are some of the assignments, named in alphabetical order, which I was involved in.

Taylor Caldwell:

I met her, a noted author who was famous for the novels she wrote. She was upset about the theft of a valuable ring worth $85,000. She even wanted her trusted staff investigated. "Put them on the lie detector!" she yelled. "Not admissible in a court of law!" was our reply to her. She was asked if she could think of anyone else who may have been responsible for the theft of her ring, and her reply was "No."

She was engaged to a man who happened to be 40 years her junior, who told her that, not only was he a former Royal Air Force pilot at one time, but he also had been engaged to one of the women from the Hearst family. I remember that when I was questioning her, he was attending to her by squeezing the pimples on her arm. (*Disgusting! I thought to myself.*)

This case was never solved, but we had an idea that he might be responsible for the theft of the ring, but we couldn't prove it. He married her and took her away to another state, thereby cutting all ties with her family. Unfortunately she died later and this left matters of her estate to be settled, which caused much concern with the family she left behind.

Vice President of the United States, Hubert Horatio Humphrey:
He is another dignitary I was lucky enough to guard "up close and personal!" He was vice president at the time of the Lyndon Johnson administration (1965-1969). During his stay here he took up residence at the Statler hotel, located in the downtown area of our city.

There was a time he came into the lobby, and I was present there and in his line of sight. I helped him down some stairs. I had him by the arm, and he in turn, reached back to help his wife descend the stairs, while we engaged in small talk.

(*I was thrilled that I was able to get this close and to speak with him!*)

Later that night there were demonstrations outside the hotel, by protesters who were against the Vietnam War. Among them were Vietnam veterans who had their medals pinned to their chests as they spoke out against the war.

The vice president left for another engagement. He returned several hours later. My partner (Joe) and I were outside when things started to get out of hand, because the crowds were screaming, "Dump the hump!" They pushed closer towards the hotel doors. We tried to hold them back, along with the uniformed personnel. At this same time the Secret Service arrived at the rear doors of the hotel with the vice president, and determined not to let him out of the car because of the aggressive nature of the crowd. He left Buffalo without further incident.

Reverend Jessie Louis Jackson:
I had the experience of guarding him. On this particular tour of duty he spoke at Kleinhans, a downtown music hall. The detail was along with the Secret Service. (*He was running for president at that time in the Democratic primary.*)

I was the only plainclothes officer on the stage with him as he spoke. When his speech was over, he backed up from the platform and stumbled. I grabbed hold of him, in the event he would fall. He then left with the secret service agents, one of whom had an Uzi under his coat (*Israel machine gun*). As they went out the door, he turned and said to me, "See you next time around."

President John F. Kennedy:

I was just a young rookie when he came to Buffalo, New York. He spoke at an outside rally at the rear of city hall (October 14, 1962). I remember looking up at this young man who was president at that time. I was assigned to the crowd, to walk around and look for any suspicious behavior which could be considered a threat.

We wanted to make sure no harm came to him because if you remember history, we gave (Buffalo did) this country two presidents (Grover Cleveland and Millard Fillmore) and took one away! (William McKinley. After McKinley's assassination, on September 6, 1901, by Leon Czolgosz, Theodore Roosevelt was then sworn as president, in Buffalo!)

I also recalled that when Kennedy left here an assassin (Lee Harvey Oswald) killed him a year later, in Dallas, Texas, on November 22, 1963.

William Kunstler:

I recalled an incident when there was a mob scene in downtown Buffalo and we were called to assist officers. Kunstler spoke at an illegal rally here. He was the lawyer for the Chicago Seven during the riots in 1968, and also for the Attica Prison rioters. He tried to provoke the crowd by telling that the state was responsible for the guards who were killed in the Attica riots.[4]

Upon arrival on the scene, we found out that there was a crowd of about four hundred persons, which occurred during the rush hour when downtown office workers left their jobs, which tended to make to matters worse. I ran up the stairs to the McKinley monument and tried to arrest him on orders of the lieutenant, but was stopped by a person who appeared to be his bodyguard. He tried to push me down the stairs, but I managed to turn aside his movement and he went down the stairs instead, which allowed Kunstler to slip away in the confusion. There was a picture of Joe and me in the university paper concerning this particular riot. If people only knew what you have to do to guard dignitaries when they come to town, because you never know when some nut might try to take a shot at them!

Policemen have an instinct about survival on the streets, like a sixth sense while doing their job. I thought I would throw this in a chapter on ESP stories which follows.

Chapter Seven
ESP

Do you believe in ESP (extra sensory perception) or unexplained circumstances which you had no control over? Listen to some of the following stories.

* * *

A Word Once Uttered Can Never Be Retracted

It was something I said at that particular time, and I don't know why, even to this day, I said what I did! I was at home, and in the process of black-topping my driveway, when a man approached me, who I knew to be the father of my next-door neighbor. As he walked over to me, he was hunched over, like he had the weight of the world on his shoulders, as he spoke to me about what was troubling him. I could feel the pain in his voice. "What can I do when the police are slow in serving a warrant on my daughter's husband?" he asked.

"The sheriff's department usually handles these family court warrants," I told him. "If they were slow in serving them, it was because they have a huge backlog of these warrants."[5] I don't know why I told him what I did when I said, "They probably wouldn't do anything unless the man took a rifle, and went over to her house and shot her." I knew that it was a terrible thing to say at this particular time, but it just came out!

I really meant if something more serious should happen, and of course, I was exaggerating, but only to make the point that at that time the police did not think of family court warrants as serious. I should have never said what I did.

To my surprise, I was amazed to learn that only several days later, the ex-husband came to the house in a taxicab with a rifle wrapped in a blanket, and killed her in front of her children. I saw her father several times after that incident, and he would shake his head and say, "You knew," leaving me with no words to express myself concerning this brutal matter which had occurred! The killer of that young woman didn't serve more than a few years in jail. I found out that he was out on the street again and people were wondering where the justice was.

So, watch what you say; Think before you speak.

* * *

There were other ESP stories which happened to me during the course of my career. So follow along as I try to give you some information about what happened in these types of situations.

* * *

I was involved in an incident which made my blood curl. I was in an unmarked car, dressed in a suit and tie, and not working undercover at that time. I spotted a man who gave me a bad feeling! I got out of my car, identified myself. and yelled to him in a loud voice, "Stop right where you are!" He froze immediately! The look on his face told me that he was dirty. I took him at gunpoint, and while feeling his waistband, I felt a gun and immediately took it from him. At the same time I put him spread eagle across the hood of my car, even though we were in the middle of traffic on a busy street.

Heavy traffic

Horns blaring

People staring

In the midst of this pandemonium, a bus driver went by, and after making eye contact with him, I gave him the high sign to call for help, i.e., putting my one hand up to my head, as if talking into a phone, which is a form of sign language. He nodded that he understood me. I stayed in this position for about two minutes, but it felt like an hour, as I stood there with a gun near this man's head, before my backup came to my assistance. How do you think

I felt being in this situation? I was frozen in time while I waited for help. I considered myself to be very lucky at this time, given the situation which had just occurred, because he could have shot me before I managed to disarm him. My instincts were right on the mark this time!

* * *

Here is another event. My partner had gone into a tavern to check out a lead, while I stayed in the car to listen to radio calls, because we did not have a portable radio.

A man came out of the tavern, who I can only describe to you as being built like a fortress, which made me think of a likeness of Mr. "T" from *The A Team*, a TV series. As he walked towards my unmarked car, I felt chills in my skin because it felt like it had pins and needles crawling inside.

I saw that he had his hand in his pocket and I think that he was touching the power of the weapon, as I have indicated previously.

Sometimes when someone carries a gun; they like
to keep their hand in their pocket
to feel it,
to feel the power,
to make sure it is still with them.

He tried to open my door! I slid across my seat to the other side and kicked it open thereby knocking him to the ground. But before he could get up he was faced with my weapon near his eyeball, which I felt was necessary. This move caught him completely off guard. I felt that he was too powerful to try to take by any other means. I searched him with my other hand and found out that there was a gun in his pocket. I put him under arrest, thereby cuffing him, just as my partner came outside and yelled, "What's going on?" He was surprised as to what just had just happened.

This man had no permit for the weapon he carried. He never saw me or my partner before, and could give no answer on why he walked up to the car the way he did. I guess I will never know the answer! He was from out of state and took the arrest without a word. Again a weird set of situations.

* * *

In yet another circumstance we were on patrol in a high-crime area of the city, when we spotted a man limping as he walked down the street. It appeared that he was trying to ignore us. I said to my partner, in jest, "He's probably got a gun taped inside his pants leg!"

We called him over to the car. As we questioned him, he was sweating and appeared to be very nervous. I ordered him to the side of the car and searched him, and much to our surprise he did in fact have a shotgun taped inside his pants leg. When questioned he indicated that he needed it for protection, because there were gang fights in the area, and he was afraid for his safety.

* * *

The next story is of a personal note, because it concerns my family. It touches me deeply, even as I am writing this. It was September of the year 2003, in which my family made the painful decision to put my younger sister, Maureen, in a nursing home. She had been an intelligent and compassionate woman, but you wouldn't know it if you had seen her then. Besides her husband, Dale, she had four children, Cheryl (who passed away at 28 years of age), Catherine, and two sons, Mark and Timothy.

She also had an identical twin sister by name of Kathleen, and two brothers, Tom and me (Mickey). Maureen suffered from Alzheimer's for a number of years. Her husband, Dale, took care of her, at a great sacrifice to both him and the extended family. Care limitations were beyond what the family could do for her, because her condition was now in a decline, which is why she ended up being placed in this nursing home. My younger brother, Tom, who was here from Atlanta, went to see her and returned home after a short visit of two days!

It was several nights after this, in which I had this eerie dream, that my sister Maureen called me on the phone and said, "Mickey, I just called to tell you that I am gone." It was several hours later when my brother called and told me that Maureen had died, which left me to wonder about the realism of dreams.

Did she call me just as she gave up her spirit?

29

In no way could we predict the series of events which were to follow, and were being dealt to us by the hand of fate. As a result we faced another tragic ordeal in its place, while the family arranged for her services. I received a phone call from my brother's daughter, Sheri, who is a doctor. She told me that her father would not be able to come to the services for Maureen, because he had gone to the hospital. He didn't feel well! He ended up having a new form of heart surgery. (He was not cut open like I was, but they went in through the ribs.) He wrote me a letter, in which he explained how he felt about this strange twist of fate! He stated that he would have surely died, had it not been for our sister (his angel), who saved his life while hers was gone. This sickness of his was apparently dormant at this time and was brought to a head because of the ordeal the family went through with Maureen.

There are numerous stories about ESP, and these were just a few of them, but I am sure you have read of other amazing events concerning this subject.

Do you believe? If so, I am sure you can recall any eerie events you may have had during your lifetime. I also had a strange experience on the death of my partner some years later, which I have narrated in the following chapter.

Chapter Eight
Joe Retires

Your Best Friend Retires!

They say you are only as good as your partner. I have to say: "I was fortunate enough to be broken in on the job by the best." He showed me the ropes when I went on an elite squad, known as the robbery squad.

Joe Schwartz was my partner for quite a number of years, starting with the robbery squad in December of 1965, and right up to when we received other assignments some eight years later.

When you read the section on the robbery squad you will be in on all the stories Joe and I faced together. We worked for some eight years and shared quite a lot of unforgettable stories, one of which had us on a death list to be assassinated, which I will relate in a later chapter.

Like Being Married

They say that working with the same partner is like being married to someone because even though we had our differences, we were great friends to the point of socializing with each other's families. When we went out drinking together, we would tell some of these stories to make ourselves laugh, because we couldn't tell them at home, as all police officers go through this in the telling their war stories.

When Joe retired, he ended up getting a nice write-up in the paper, along with his picture, and a big party. The following is a quote from the newspaper about Joe's retirement party, in which the article declared: "Big Joe Schwartz is hanging up his shield and gun today after a 24-year record of bank robbery arrests and commendations. He joined the police force after three years with the Navy Seabees and nine years with Bethlehem Steel Co. He worked for 15 years on the robbery squad and covered more than 100 bank robberies as well as other armed robberies."

Big Cigar

I spoke about him to various people. He was a hell of a nice person. His trademark was a big cigar in his mouth. This irked the chief of detectives, who thought it distorted Joe's TV image when he appeared on the news programs.

We appeared on the evening news frequently relative to current crime events!

Even some of the criminal elements liked him. There was one guy who called Joe up on the phone and asked him if he should cut his hair when he came down to the area we worked because he didn't want Joe mad at him.

Joe was kind, in that if someone was in need, he would help. I remembered one incident, when a couple who gave us much-needed information received a washer and a dryer from him, which he knew they needed. We used to have to pay informants out of our own pocket, unless it was a big case, then we would have to clear it with the chief of detectives before acquiring more money.

* * *

Respect from Patrol Officers

The patrol officers respected us because we used to respond to hot calls to back them up, since we knew that the patrol force was the backbone of the police department! As you will see in other stories, we received several awards from the police officers' organization.

Cancer

It is with deep sadness that I have to tell you that my partner Joe lived under the threat of cancer, and was in the hospital, and then a nursing home. I went to see him there and we exchanged these war stories which are in this book, and believe me, we had a great time laughing about them.

Warned Me of My Food

I remember a time at the hospital when I was helping him with his food. He gave me a banana, and then took it back and said, "Wait until I cut the bad part out, you don't want to eat that part!" This left you to feel that he was thoughtful, even though he lived with his burden of facing possible death.

The last time I saw him alive was the first week of January 1999. He died the next week. I wished I could have spent more quality time with him before he passed away.

It Was Opened to That Page

I learned of his death in an unusual way, because I was in a restaurant and was thinking about when I could go see him next, when I happened to glance at a paper which was lying nearby, and it was open to the obituary section. There was Joe's picture! He had died! (Weird.)

I went to his wake and noticed that the family had his scrapbook out on a table near his coffin, and foremost were the pictures of Joe and me, and the head of the FBI, featured in the local paper about us chasing bank robbers to Rochester. This picture made me feel sad, upon looking at it, and I had to exit the funeral parlor at that time, because of the memories it brought up.

He was a great partner and a good friend. I shall miss him.

The following story is one of the bigger cases which he and I were in on.

This drew headlines from the media because of who the killer was. Follow along and you will see what I mean.

Chapter Nine
Kitty Genovese! Who Was She?

Kitty Genovese was famous too. This is about a case on TV which became a subject of public indifference. I used her name first because her murder gained more notoriety than her killer did. If by chance you did not see it on TV, or even read about it, the following story will refresh your memory.

Who was she? The answer to that question is she was the victim of a murder. A man named Winston Moseley killed her on March 13, 1964, in New York City, while 38 people watched from an apartment complex, as he stabbed her over and over again.

They even continued watching when he came back to the scene to finish her off. There was not one phone call made to the police. I am telling you this because I was involved with her killer in a case here in Buffalo. I was studying at Buffalo State College in the '80s and read about her in a philosophy book.[6]

It made me recall my part in the apprehension of this man who was her killer. Moseley was taken to the then Meyer Hospital (now ECMC) in Buffalo, New York, for a self-inflicted wound. He stuck an open-ended can of tomato juice up his rectum, because he knew that the prison authorities could not handle this emergency. He then managed to escape from his one guard by asking to go to the bathroom and then while inside he climbed out a window to make good his escape.[7]

Moseley broke into a nearby residence and stayed there for four days. He met a cleaning woman whom he talked into running away with him, and asked her to bring him clothes and money. But later he was discovered by a man and a woman who were relatives of the person who owned the house.

It was at this time that he committed the crime of raping the woman and forcing her husband to watch while holding a gun to them. (*He found the gun in the house.*) Afterwards he took the keys to their car and left the scene of this crime, leaving the victim in a horrified condition.

This is when my partner Joe Schwartz and I entered the picture. It was our job to investigate the assault and rape of this victim, here in Buffalo. We came up with the lead in this case because we figured that it could possibly be the man who had fled the hospital. We showed his mug photo to the victims, along with other mugs so as not to jeopardize any future case. "That's him!" they said.

Meanwhile, Moseley drove to Grand Island, just outside of Buffalo. He picked out a series of apartments, rang a doorbell, and forced himself in at gunpoint. Once inside, he held two women and a baby there. He allowed one of the women to pick up her children at school. (Odd?)

This is when she alerted the FBI, which caused them to get involved. They set up a command post, and began to figure out how they could catch Moseley, who was still in the woman's apartment, with a hostage. FBI agent Neil J. Welch talked to Moseley on the telephone and persuaded him to let him into the apartment. Moseley surrendered to Welch. Welch would later write a book titled *Inside Hoover's FBI*, in which he touches on Moseley's arrest.

We had worked with him on other occasions, because this is the same agent who went with us to Rochester to capture a bank robbery suspect. He was one of the few men picked to replace Hoover in the director's job in Washington, but politics took its course and he did not get the job, even though most people thought that he was well qualified to take over the reins. This is how Joe and I got in on the capture of Winston Moseley. We were right outside the window, when Agent Welch captured him and came outside of the apartments.

The local newspaper wrote the story up this way, "That during the time of his court appearance, Moseley, who appeared extremely alert, was handcuffed to two police officers. He was handcuffed on the left hand to Detective Michael J. Chernetsky, and on the right hand to Detective Joseph A. Schwartz, both of the robbery squad."

Another article in the newspaper brings up the trauma this woman, who was the victim of rape, went through, especially while in the police car with Joe and me. The article was in a New York City daily newspaper dated December 1, 1969, which talked about a 1.25 million-dollar negligence suit filed by the victim in this case.

Another feature, written on April 1, 1997, stated that while in jail, Moseley becomes a graduate, with state aid, as he earns his master's degree, for which he can collect several more thousand dollars in state aid. Do you get this? Now he becomes a graduate student and ends up with a master's degree with our tax dollars (TAP tuition assistance program). Let me say this, after all of the time and money spent taking up our blocked court system, just who are the real victims here? Perhaps, we the public, i.e. you the reader, should keep asking ourselves this question before we are quick to have all these appeals justified in the defense of the aforementioned criminals. I also wonder what the Genovese family and the victims in our Buffalo case would say relative to this question.

In another coincidence, my father's sister married a Genovese and they lived in New York City at that time; however, there was no relation to this Kitty Genovese. *Now that you know who she was, do you remember the story on TV?*

You're making all these arrests, but what happens when someone doesn't want to go with you and you know you can't shoot them? Follow the next chapter on self-defense.

Chapter Ten
Know Something!

What happens if you are suddenly attacked? Do you know something? This is a term used on the street! This means that you can defend yourself or another person if necessary. This will make a person cautious of you, even if it's a street fight, barehanded, or with a knife, or some other means of self-defense.

Some people think, since you have a badge and a gun, you can always shoot someone if the going gets rough. This is not the case because you cannot just rely on your weapon. The average person arrested thinks that they might chance it by fighting with you, knowing that you can't shoot them, because they know the law as well as you do. They feel that you are ignorant as to who they are, and will take this risk to prevent you from taking them in, where their identity will be uncovered and become a public record. They could be a person who is wanted and this would give them a good reason to resist arrest by any means, even by taking your life.

Of course there are cases when the person you are trying to arrest could be a mental case, or they could be on drugs, in which case they would have amazing strength thereby making it extremely difficult to handcuff them.

Do you think it is easy to handcuff someone? The public thinks that it is easy to handcuff a suspect and take him or her in without a fuss. They say, "You carry a gun, and it should be no problem to carry out this duty. You are trained in that stuff! It should be a snap." In reality, if the individual doesn't want to go, and you have to fight, it's tough to do so without hurting anyone, especially when they are putting up a fierce struggle to get away, as I indicated in this aforementioned incident.

You don't want to hurt someone but at the same time, you want to go home in one piece. When you get a little up on age, you have to go with the flow. As some smart street cops used to say to one another, "Be careful, it's a jungle out there."

Defending yourself to keep from being hurt or beaten up is one thing, but to handcuff someone who does not wish to go, and holding him down without hurting him is an entirely different set of circumstances. Trust me on this!

In that split second of time, when the action started, some people judge you for what you did, and they have months to study it, to see if you did it right. But you only have that one split second to decide just how much force is necessary or allowed.

You don't want to be known as a cop with notches on his gun with reference to persons he killed while on the job. I knew of a few officers who bore this load on their shoulders. Or look at it this way, suppose you have killed someone, and then you are confronted with a like situation. You may be hesitant, and get yourself, or someone that you are protecting, killed.

As a young police officer and a detective who was a good street cop, I knew how to defend myself. I studied sport judo for four years before I came on the police department. At first, I studied in Canada, as they had no judo clubs in the Buffalo area. I joined up at the downtown YMCA in Buffalo when they started one up in this city. I used to fight in judo matches across New York State.

I still have a reminder of one such match. An opponent tried to throw me over his shoulder, and I countered with a thrust of my hips to lift him in the air, but he threw his head back, and head-butted me below the right eye. This left me with a scar in my right eyebrow, which I have to this day.

I remember that a black belt judo instructor once told me a phrase that I won't forget, "It's not the size of the dog in the fight but the fight in the dog."

* * *

Let me tell about another situation when I was working on the undercover squad, and had to use a judo throw to protect myself, and it ended up unsuccessful. An individual was attacking me, and I threw myself to the ground and put my foot into his stomach to fling him over my head to the pavement behind me. However, "Murphy's Law"[8] kicked in, and I ended up with him on top of me instead, with my gun jamming into the center of my back and knocking the wind out of me. I told myself that I would never go down onto my back, or wear my gun there in that position again, because if it had gone off, it would have shot me in the ass.

I tried to break into the wrestling game. I figured that since I knew the judo moves and could break my fall while being thrown through the air, that I could also wrestle. I joined a team of wrestlers who were in training at a local gym. Part of the deal was to sign a contract with my trainer, who was also wrestling in the ring. +

I wrestled in quite a few exhibition matches.

I was working with a wrestler who was also inexperienced too. He was supposed to kick the mat next to my head, but missed and kicked me right in the eye instead. I bled all over the place and they carried me out of the ring. Because of this incident I have a scar in my left eyebrow!

As the years went by, the street people became more aware of karate moves by watching all the movies on TV, leaving everybody wanting to have some cool karate moves! While I was still on the department, and was in my late thirties, I studied karate from two different masters. This was only for three months each time, because I couldn't afford to continue the lessons.

Additionally, you should watch what you wear when you are in a fight!

I remember one incident when I fought this large man, and knocked him to the pavement. I was standing over him to try to handcuff him, when he just reached up and grabbed my necktie, and began choking me to the point that I almost lost consciousness before I was able to bring him under control and handcuff him. I must say that you can bet that I learned from this experience and only wore clip-on ties after.

* * *

There was another experience when I went to the aid of a fallen police officer because of the fact that this attacker was kicking him in the head while he was down on the ground.

I started to take my gun out of its holster, but then I realized that I could not shoot, for fear of hitting bystanders. I leaped in the air, to give this man a karate kick in the head, to save this officer's life. I soon found out that I made a mistake because unknown to me this person was a karate expert.

Much to my surprise he caught me in midair and body slammed me to the concrete. My background in judo saved me from obtaining damage to my back, as I was able to turn in the air and to break my fall.

I still managed to get up right away to continue the fight, thus piercing him in the eyes and then kicking him in the groin. (This may sound horrible, but he was trying to kill a cop!)

He was not the only one involved, due to the fact that we not only fought with him, but also his two friends.

At this moment, a young uniformed officer approached me, and I noticed that he had a gun in his hand, and he said to me, "Is this your gun, sir?" I then noticed my empty holster and replied, "Yes, it is!" It flew out as I leaped in the air. Thank God that no one else picked the gun up from the pavement.

The result was that all three men were booked for the assault on the first officer. A year later, according to a write-up in the newspapers, the first man paid a fine due to reduced charges, and the other two had pled guilty before this.

Maybe now you have a different opinion on street fighting and the responsibility officers have in trying to defend themselves and others.

So, if you should witness a scuffle on the street, think about how would you handle it? Now that you have read this do you know something? Maybe you never got in a fight in your life! Could you handle an attack upon your person?

Some officers are sued for what they did on the job but how about being sued for something you didn't do. Follow along and you will find out as I did when I was sued while on the job, for not doing something!

Chapter Eleven
Lawsuit

Have you ever been sued? Or has this happened in your family, the result of which dealt an economic blow to them. Well, this happened to me near the end of my career! This unpleasant occurrence was because of a complainant, who launched an $11 million lawsuit against me.

But why did he do it? It was because of advice given to him by people who were supposed to be on my side of the bar of justice.

Here is how it all started! I was trying to do the right thing, when I picked up my caseload as usual and proceeded to investigate a crime of assault.

In this case a man came to a house in the early hours of the morning, with the intention of hurting his girlfriend, and while inside he attacked her. Her cousin came to her assistance, and this person took a ten-pound barbell weight and bashed the cousin's head in before he fled the house. I managed to piece together the circumstances concerning this crime when I took up the investigation. I learned that the assailant had made prior crime reports, which were false, concerning this same address. Unknown to me, he returned to this house sometime later in the day, and again attempted to attack this same young woman, whom he accused of sleeping with some of the men in the house. At this time, remembering what had happened earlier, several men in the house tried to prevent him from getting at her again, thereby throwing him off the property by means of the front porch.

I managed to get statements from all witnesses, including these two men, thereby obtaining warrants for this same man, and on November 30, 1992, we arrested him on the basis of the warrant. He was then convicted after standing trial, and sent to prison for one year, of which he only served four months for this serious assault.

During his time in prison, he continued to harass me by sending me letters in which he demanded to know why I had not arrested the two men who had prevented him from reentering that house. Not only did he send me letters, but he also sent letters to a female warrant clerk, thereby harassing her as well!

Upon his release, he went after the same warrant clerk verbally. He was referred to the DA's (district attorney) office, who in turn decided that I should issue warrants for the two men who threw him off the porch.

In his mind, he believed that it was the right thing to do because he had spoken with people in the DA's office, who advised him in that direction. They told him that this situation was my fault and sent him over to my office. They even had the nerve to call me on the telephone saying, "Sarge! Deal with this. He's your problem, not ours." I refused to do so, and went over the particulars, letters and all. I said, "In a good sense of right and wrong I would not issue warrants for those two men, as they were defending the woman who was in the earlier incident. Why should I give them a record?" I told those in the DA's office who were trying to push this arrest on me. I went on to say that the assailant tried to return to the house in question to finish the job he started earlier, i.e. assault the female. But this fell on deaf ears as they didn't want to be bothered with hearing these facts, because they didn't want to ruffle the man's feathers but ended up giving him encouragement and told him to see me about this matter because they didn't want a complaint against them. It is a good thing that I kept copies of the letters he sent me. I wrote notes on when he came to the station house and harassed me and other officers, upon which he ended up being physically removed out of the station house when he would not leave, as ordered to do so by the desk officers.

Can you believe this? I was then served with papers, which then launched this ridiculous lawsuit against me, for $11 million, costing time and money to the state, and again causing me and my family unnecessary anxiety. I handed over all the material I had relative to this case to our corporation counsel to prepare her for the trial. I also made out numerous reports on the previous events leading up to this case and afterwards.

In January (1993) the US District Court dismissed this lawsuit, and you know as well as I do, that it never should have gotten this far; it could have been stopped back at square one where it started. Next time you want to sue someone think of the cost on both sides of the fence before you are talked into it by some attorney who wants notoriety or capital gain.

* * *

How do you handle someone who has strength and doesn't know what he or she is doing? What should you do? In keeping with my alphabetical format, the next series explains some incidents of the mentally retarded offender.

Chapter Twelve
The Mentally Retarded Offender

How does one go about treating the person who commits a felony crime and does not know why he or she is doing it, or have the mental capacity to know right from wrong concerning this matter? The persons themselves and the persons that take care of these individuals hold this opinion of not having responsibility.

The following case is about such an incident, followed by other related cases pertaining to to this subject.

I thought about this problem of the mentally retarded offender when I wrote a paper for a class entitled "The Introduction to Mental Retardation," taught by Dr. R. B. Baum, of the State University College at Buffalo, while I was still on the Buffalo Police Department. This paper was about a case I investigated.

* * *

Who Knows Their State of Mind?

In the following case there was a mildly retarded adult who committed a crime, which caused me to think about that paper. It was during the time I was in the process of booking him. I was assigned to this case, and would find out it was more involved than anyone could have expected. It began the following way.

I went to the address mentioned on the police report, and questioned the victim, a 28-year-old schoolteacher. She said, "I only left my apartment for a few days and when I got back I found out that it had been broken into." As I left her apartment, both the property owner and John Doe confronted me. I discussed the situation with both of them.

I returned to the station house and directed my attention to other investigations which merited my attention during the remainder of the day. I was not able to continue on this case for several days, because at that time we had to investigate some 20 or more cases a day. We took the most serious cases first.

It was several days later when I was able to speak to the victim and property owner again. I also questioned some of the neighbors. I found out that John Doe's name kept coming up. People said that he was a strange man, suspected of starting several fires in the neighborhood, and that he looked into bedroom windows at night. According to them, it was learned that a young woman, who used to live in the same apartment where the burglary occurred, said that John Doe climbed into her bedroom window and jumped into bed with her, causing her to move out. She did not want to press charges against him.

In this most recent case the victim obtained her property back. John Doe told her that he found it in the garbage. This left me to wonder whether or not it had any damage after being exposed to the elements because it had snowed the night before. I asked her if she thought it showed damage by being out in the weather. Her reply was no, that it wasn't wet.

I then paid John Doe a visit. I went to his apartment and rang the doorbell. After receiving no response I decided to go to the rear of the house to knock on his back window. But before I could do so, he opened his door, thereby allowing me to enter. I identified myself as a police officer, even though he knew who I was from my previous conversations with him.

I looked around the apartment and spotted a TV, which looked like the one stolen from the victim's apartment. I advised him of his rights and proceeded to question him. I was not surprised by his answer, when he told me that he found the TV in the garbage outside of his house. I wanted to verify the TV's serial number with the one from the burglary report, and called my office, and they in turn gave me the information I needed. It matched!

I probably should have charged him with burglary, but decided to charge him with stolen property instead. I would let the courts decide on the merits of the burglary charge, because in my mind, it was his state of mind, relative to his actions concerning this matter. I told him that I was not going to hurt him, but I would have to put handcuffs on him and took the time to explain to him that it was necessary. He agreed to let me handcuff him. (I had a fear that he might jump out of the police car while on the way to the station house!)

We left the house, with him walking a few steps ahead of me, while I carried the stolen TV. The neighbors watched this strange procession. I took him to the station house and proceeded to book him in accordance with a violation of the New York State Penal Code. I pondered the thought of why I didn't charged him with the crime of burglary, as he had admitted it. All the necessary words of the proper law flashed through my mind, intent, benefit, culpability, possession, and control. I still doubted how far to push this, because I had already made up my mind to do the right thing by him. But things were, going his way anyway

The complainant in this case did not show up in court.

I called her house to find out why, and she stated that she did not want to pursue this matter any further, because she liked him and did not want to cause him any harm.

The social worker was present and she couldn't believe that he would confess this crime to me, let alone even do such a thing.

The family was present and they were delighted when the judge dismissed charges against him, as was his lawyer.

John Doe was present. He saw me outside of the courtroom, came over to me and shook my hand, before he joined his family in conversation.

I could not bring this up in court at this time, but he had a previous arrest record. He appeared before the court system on other occasions, where he received a slap on the wrist. I saw him several years later on the street and he remembered me. He came up to the police car, shook my hand, and engaged me in an extensive conversation.

* * *

Here are some other cases which involved the mentally challenged

Female Assailant Cuts Face

Prior to writing this report, I had to arrest a mentally retarded female, which acquired the assistance of a policewoman. The assailant felt that she did not do anything wrong, and neither did the person responsible for her care and welfare.

A Piece of Paper

We solved this case with just a piece of paper with a phone number on it.[9] This was given to us after we found out that the bartender aided in the escape of the attacker in this case. We told him, "Do you realize the trouble you will be in by withholding this information?"

The assailant in this case was a white female, age 33, who cut this young girl's face with a beer bottle. It required 77 stitches to close the wounds in her face. It was because this woman didn't like the idea that someone had called her friend some names.

Another woman, who thought that she was doing the right thing, confronted me and told me that she ran a home for two of these clients. She said, "I am duty-bound to protect my clients, even by hiding them from the police, no matter what crimes they may have committed."

I think that her custodian should share some of the blame in this by covering this up.

In this particular circumstance, the courts will have to decide just what went on inside that woman's head, when she cut this young woman's face, particularly since she had two prior arrests for assaults, which could not be brought up during the trial.

He Landed in the Wrong Territory

In this case we answered a radio call, "Man with a gun," on a busy city parkway. Upon our arrival, we noticed a man in the middle of the street who had an empty holster on his belt and was in some sort of combat uniform. We decided to check him out further. He said to us, "I am on a secret mission! Look in my swimming trunks. I have a map for my assignment, if you don't believe me."

Secret Map

We had him take off his pants and his shirt and noted that he had navy-type swimming trunks on underneath. Inside the pocket of the swimming trunks was a laminated map folded up very neatly. He went on to say, "I landed as a paratrooper in the wrong place. Here is my military ID's." We made copies of them, and then we locked him up in a cell for safekeeping. The DA told us that they had called the Veterans Administration and his counselors were coming over.

* * *

In yet another situation a woman came to us for help in serving a mental hygiene warrant on her son. "Be cautious," she said. "The last time there was a struggle with the police officers who were enforcing a previous warrant." She opened the lower door for us. At this time we noticed a sign, which read: "Police do not enter!"

He greased the stairs with lard, so that we would slip and fall while trying to go up. At the top, there was a small table with two lit candles on it, along with a picture of him in a military uniform. He had barricaded himself in the bathroom. We called to him by name and received no response even though we knocked on the door and made our presence known.

We heard clicks

We were about to take down the door when we heard the sound of a gun's trigger being cocked backward, and it was at that time that I thought to myself, *My God, I really don't want to shoot someone who is mentally ill, and I surely didn't want to be killed by one either.*

Hold Your Fire!

We took down the door and learned that the clicks we heard was the sound of him trying to open his pill bottle. There he was, kneeling on the bathroom floor, with tears flowing down his cheeks. We took him in, so that he could get the help he needed, and thanked God it ended up this way, without anyone getting hurt, because after all, we were only serving a warrant at the request of the family.

In closing I wish to say that the answer will not only be in the courts but people will have to decide what, if anything, can be done about the handling of the mentally retarded offender and what to do when they are placed in prison with the general population.

* * *

There are times when you will be confronted with dead bodies and it isn't pretty. There is a specialized squad that handles this but here you are, first on the scene.

Follow along as we are confronted with the crime of murder.

Chapter Thirteen
Murder

Murder! There were times that we came across homicides before the specialized unit arrived on the scene. The following cases are examples.

Murder by Execution

We received a call from concerned parents who had not heard from their daughter in a while. We went to where the girl lived, along with her parents and the property owner of the premises. We knocked on the door, but received no response. We asked the landlord to open the door. "I won't do that," he replied, "and if you break it down you will have to pay for it." We broke down the door to her apartment! There was her body on the floor, with her hands tied behind her back, along with a bullet in the back of her head: execution style. A blindfold was over her eyes and it appeared that she was forced into a kneeling position!

Several days later, after further investigation by the homicide unit, her boyfriend ended up charged in this brutal murder.

* * *

Serial Killer Loose

This next case brought daily headlines! It caused great concern in the black community, not only in Buffalo, New York, but in the suburbs as well. People were afraid to go about their daily business for fear that they too would become a victim of the so-called .22-Cal Killer, who was on the loose and was only targeting black people.

Grim Reaper

The city was in panic! As if a large figure of the Grim Reaper hovered over it! This made people so on edge that the average black person was suspicious of everybody.

My involvement in this tragic event was slight. It was homicide case! They asked for assistance from other detectives, so we were involved in some leads. I was working on the case along with many other detectives who devoted extra hours to catch this vicious killer.

The first victim of the .22-Cal Killer was in a supermarket parking lot where I usually worked in an off-duty capacity; however, I was working at another location when it occurred. The victim happened to be a 14-year-old black youth, who was seated in a car when the .22-Cal Killer came up and shot him in the head.

Must Be Him

There was a friend of mine who worked in a hot precinct when the composite went out of the description of this killer which was published in the newspapers. It looked similar to this detective.[10] He was walking to work, and was set upon by a group of citizens who surrounded him because they thought that he was the killer. They held him at bay until the police came to his rescue.

Thank God they didn't shoot him first and ask questions later.

There was an incident that happened at one of the funerals, when gangs of white men in cars taunted the mourners and drove away. This troubled us, leading us to believe that perhaps more individuals were involved in this particular case. Persons at this funeral were only able to give an unclear description of the cars involved and no one was able to get a license plate number.

We came upon weird people during the course of this investigation. One of whom was a white man who had a picture of the Son of Sam on his mantle.[11] There were two candles lit on either side of the picture, as if it was a shrine. He also carried a vial on his belt, with toenail clippings, along with pubic hairs that he took from his girlfriend.

I am sure you heard of copycat killers. They use the description of the MO (method of operation) used by the actual killer. A few individuals used this crime wave to gain notoriety for themselves by proclaiming that they too, were the victim of the .22-Cal Killer, stating that they fought him off and got away from him.

The papers all played up the capture of the .22-Cal Killer! The only reason his capture came about was that while in the Army, he received a stab wound in a fight, and, while in the hospital, he was bragging about killing blacks in Buffalo. The state police were notified and began an investigation, which led to their investigators searching his home and a cabin in the woods. Because of the .22-Cal Killer's capture, a twist of fate in this case came about.

I was just returning from Toronto with my family. This was a hard pill to swallow because it must be mentioned that after all the time and effort I put into this case, that this guy lived just three doors away from a house I had just moved into. Can you believe this?

I was embarrassed on where he was located, especially when I recalled watching state police investigators going to his house which was only a few doors from where I now lived, and was clueless as to what was going on at this time. It wasn't because of the capture, in which I was glad that someone got him, but this peculiarity of fate, on where he happened to reside. I worked on this case, along with others, for months, and took a ribbing on the outcome.

The .22-Cal Killer was identified as Joseph C. Christopher. He died in prison, at the age of 37, in 1993.

* * *

Second Chance to Kill Again

In still another case there was a brutal murder of a young girl. The worst part of this case is that the man just got out on parole for a crime in which he tried to kill another woman a month after he got out from a correctional facility. He only served three years on that crime. In the most recent crime he had gone to the victim's house with the intention of looking at a bike which was for sale, and which she had advertised in the paper. He would return and kill her in a ghastly way.

Almost Decapitated

Her mother discovered her grotesque nude body in an upstairs bedroom, when she arrived home. Her daughter was almost decapitated, leaving her mother in a state of agony after seeing her that way.

I was working alone on that particular day, and was one of the first detectives to arrive on the scene. I happened to talk to the officer who called me to the crime scene. As I approached the doorway, this officer, who I knew as "Don," said to me, "It's a bad one, Mike," and went on to explain to me what happened.[12]

I went upstairs to her room and looked at the horrible sight of her head almost decapitated. I bowed my head and said a little prayer

"Don't worry, honey; we'll get the guy who did this to you."

The chief of homicide arrived on the scene, and carefully bagged her hands. This was police procedure in the event there was any skin from the killer underneath her fingernails.

We pieced the preceding events together, and a description of the suspect emerged as a result of the memory of this particular officer. Don said, "I might know who did this. It is a guy who just got out of jail." Don came back later with the name of this individual. The fingerprints found on the back of the bedroom door matched the name of the suspect that he named! (Good work, Don!) I want to mention at this time that I knew Don from working on the vice squad. He was a very knowledgeable officer, and was well liked by all persons who came in contact with him. He also worked with me on a second front, another job which consisted of driving a package truck for a downtown delivery service. I had been over to his home on a few occasions. I even recall watching the debut of the Beatles when they first came to America while visiting Don's house.

There are times when you might have to take a few punches and not lock anyone up, as you have to put yourself in that person's shoes. This happened to me when the victim's brother came upon the crime scene. I was at the door, but I wouldn't let him in, saying to him, "You don't want to remember her this way." I blocked his entrance to the house. This caused him to kick and punch me to get in. I could not press charges in this matter because I felt deep sympathy for his anxiety at this moment of his life.

The murderer was arrested. Additional background information came up with the fact that after the killer had murdered this young girl, he went to his sister's house, and washed his bloody clothes in her washer.

A local paper said, "This time the killer was permitted to plead guilty to a reduced charge." He did not want to make the same mistake twice, i.e. when he attacked this most recent girl, and that's why he wanted to make sure that she was dead. Because of the higher court ruling and an insanity defense, prosecutors, in an effort to save this case, allowed the defendant to plead guilty to a manslaughter charge. He went before the Supreme Court, which caused him to receive only a sentence of 12 years to 25 years. The family has to go through more pain and suffering because this killer applied for parole in 1999.

* * *

In yet another case, we answered a call of a dead body in an upstairs apartment. Upon arrival at the scene, we noticed a group of men playing cards in the kitchen, as if nothing happened. When we looked around the premises in another area of the house, we spotted a man seated upright in a chair, with his blood all over the floor, which had drained out of him.

No one had helped him, or was aware of how this happened to him. Further investigation by homicide disclosed that it was no murder, but that he came home drunk, walked up the stairs, leaving a trail of blood, thereby collapsing in the chair in which we found him. He must have slipped while he was going up the stairs, and a bottle opener (or what some call a church key) which was in his side pocket had gone into his artery, causing him to bleed to death.

Things were not always what they appear to be as in this particular case!

Homicide investigators deserve all the respect for the job they do in hunting down this human animal who kills other people. I wrote a poem about this which is in another chapter.

There are times when you are going to be in situations, but you are off duty. What happens then? Find out in the next chapter!

Chapter Fourteen
Off Duty

According to the police department, you are never off duty, because you are supposed to be carrying your gun at all times, and should an occasion arise, which is of a serious nature, and committed in your presence, you are supposed to act. *I have to add this thought, that in addition, someone in authority has two or three months to decide whether or not you acted properly.*

The following incidents happened while off duty and as such we were compelled to act upon what we saw.

* * *

Wanted? FBI List!

Joe and I were off duty and unwinding in a tavern when this man walked in. He looked like one of the wanted posters we had seen previously.

One of us always carried mug shots and sometimes even the FBI's most wanted list.

We took this picture out and showed it to the bartender. He responded with, "Yeah, I would say he sure looks like the picture. I never saw him before." We sat there and figured that our man would have to go to the bathroom eventually, or we would get him as he leaves the premises. We decided to wait him out. He finally went into the bathroom, followed by us, and just as he was going to take a leak, he found himself staring down two guns. It was at this time that my partner said, "Just keep right on pissing" as we told him that we were both police officers and displayed our badges.

After checking his identification and looking for the tattoos which he was supposed to have, and finding none, we discovered that we made a mistake.

After we showed him the picture, he even agreed with us that he looked like the man, and we figured that he was glad that no one got an itchy trigger finger while he was taking a leak.

* * *

You might have to make an arrest while you are off duty, which happened to me on more than one occasion, as indicated in the following stories. How about seizing a man with a gun, while off duty, and then finding out later that there was another man with a gun nearby? These stories add credibility to the advice given to us by some old-timers, who used to say to us rookies: "You'll never find crime in church."

* * *

Lost His Gun!

In this occurrence, Joe and I were having a few brews in a local tavern while we were off duty. We noticed this man moving chairs around in a hurried fashion, as if he lost something important! We looked at his belt, and noticed the empty holster. We realized at the same time that he must have lost his gun. "That's what he was looking for," we said to one another. We got to the gun before he did. We discovered that he didn't have a permit for it, so we arrested him and took him downtown for booking.

Afterwards we decided to return to the same tavern. As soon as we arrived there, a barmaid said to us, "Did you get the second guy?"

"What second person?" we asked. She then pointed to a man who now was quickly going out the door. We chased him out onto the street and upon searching him we found out that he was also carrying a gun and had no permit for it and placed him under arrest.

Thank God that he didn't shoot us when we arrested his friend.

They both remarked upon being booked, "Do you think that we are crazy to come down in this section without a gun for protection?"

We looked at it this way; we took two guns off the street!

* * *

Not Funny

The following incident occurred while we both were in a popular downtown restaurant. My partner noticed the expression on my face change! I was in the process of drawing my gun, and pointing it in his direction. "What are you doing?" he asked. What he didn't know, was that a man who was seated behind us pulled a gun and was holding it at a 90-degree angle and was in the process of leveling it towards my partner's head.

"Drop the gun," I yelled, as I stood up and pointed my 9mm towards his head. I almost fired my weapon to protect my partner. The weapon he was pointing at my partner's head was an imitation pistol, which was a cigarette lighter, and looked like a small derringer. He was trying to be amusing, and said he found the whole thing very funny. My partner and I didn't, because we locked him up on a charge of an imitation pistol.

* * *

He Wasn't Kidding

We were off duty in a local restaurant, talking about the job, as most cops do because you can't tell your stories at home. One of our friends, a fellow detective, was at the end of the bar. He was drinking with someone we did not know.

All of a sudden the person he was in a conversation with leaps up on the bar, pulls out a large butterfly knife, and charges towards us, screaming, "I'm going to kill you!" We pulled our guns out, and were ready to shoot him, as we tilted our chairs back, due to the fact that he was on top of the bar and now was hovering over us, waving his knife. (Can you picture this?)

We disarmed him without any further trouble. We could have shot him right there, in self-defense. It seemed that during the course of the conversation he was telling our friend that he hated us, that he was going to kill us, as he motioned down the bar towards us, but our friend thought he was only kidding around.

* * *

Just Going to the Store!

My kids won't ever forget this experience! I left the house for the purpose of going to the store for a newspaper. As I rounded the corner of our street, I noticed a few of our officers lying in the grass with their guns drawn. They recognized me and explained that they couldn't get back to their car, as they were covering the front of a house, where they saw a man who is wanted for murder enter. They figured they were not seen, so they just decided to stay were they were. The one officer stated that he did not have a portable radio to alert our radio dispatcher, when they spotted this guy enter the house which was a short distance away. I informed them that I would take care of it. I went back to my house and put on my bulletproof vest, put on my 9mm Glock, and left the house with my family looking on in total puzzlement.

I called radio again, but this time from their patrol car and informed the dispatcher who I was, and that I was the same person who called them from the phone. I made sure that my name and rank went over the air. I did this to make sure I was covered insurance-wise in the event something should happen to me.

The assistant chief of detectives called out the SWAT team. He sent them to the house in which the suspect was believed to have gone. We all held our ground until they arrived, and watched them surround the area and then enter the house in question. They found out, from the persons inside, that our man had slipped away earlier. It may have been that he spotted the patrol units who first saw him. It was later determined that he was in fact the person who they saw enter the house.

Some weeks later, he went to court and was tried and convicted for the many crimes he committed! In fact, even while he was in prison he made phone calls and was directing his operation and reign of terror from his cell.

I investigated some of those cases in which he threatened to kill people while using the prison telephone system. His lawyer had the nerve to cite the court and complain that this was a violation of his client's rights because of the monitoring of his phone calls even though the man was planning crimes from his jail cell.

Guess who else was in the house?

The man I arrested three times previously was in this house. Remember this was mentioned in an article named "Nemesis," carried in the local newspapers. However there was no arrest this time, and I want to say that this was the fourth time our paths would cross. *This was an eerie feeling!*

* * *

Hide in Plain Sight!

There is a movie called *Hide in Plain Sight*, staring James Caan, which played here in Buffalo in 1978, based on real-life characters ,some of whom I knew.

This movie was about a mobster who was convicted of holding up the treasurer's office in the city of Buffalo, New York. He was placed in the witness protection program, even though he was with a woman who had taken her three children from her husband and went to live with this gangster. [13] The government didn't care about the father of the children; all they cared about was that they got good information against the mob from this individual.

It was a heart-wrenching story about this father's plight to get his children back and in essence kidnapped by the government, because they would not tell him where his kids were.

However, did you know that Tom Leonard (the subject of this movie) came to my house looking for his kids? My ex- wife, at that time, stated that she did not know their whereabouts. (She knew the woman who took the children.) She had no idea that this person she once knew could be involved with this individual.

I was privy to this part of the story through my contacts in the department and thought it was cruelty by the government in the highest level. I talked to some of the detectives that were guarding this guy while he was in Buffalo, and they didn't seem to care about the kids, as one of the detectives informed me.

"Just look at the big picture He is supplying us with good information and no one can know where he is. It's not our fault that some woman decided to be with him, and happened to bring her kids along." The government even gave this guy a gun and let him work security details in various states. They later found out about an arrest for larcenies he committed while being protected by the government and of course they didn't know it at the time and were humiliated.

Tom Leonard searched for his children for years before he finally got them back and the final ending was in the papers.

* * *

Thought He Had a Bad Guy!

I was off duty with my wife and children in a large department store. I noticed that the security guard was paying too much attention to me. It was my thought at that time that he may have spotted the bulge in my jacket, because of the service revolver I was carrying. "Step away from me," I told my wife and kids.

As I watched, I saw him motion to some other security officers, who were in uniform. He talked to them for a few minutes and it appeared that they were both looking in my direction. It was at this moment that the guard now approached me directly. I noticed that it appeared that he might draw his weapon, as he had his arm hanging down in a Wyatt Erp fashion. "Let's see some identification," he yelled at me.

"I have a badge in my left coat pocket," I said. Instead of taking me at my word and telling me that he was only doing his job here in the store, he became angry and stormed away.

I happened to speak to officers in the mall, and they informed me that he spoke to them and said, "There is a guy in the store that I think is some kind of gangster and I am going to take him down. Cover me!"

* * *

Whom Do You Trust?

You never know who you can trust when you are dealing with criminals. Sometimes you believe them, and other times you have to be suspicious because they are just telling you what they think that you want to hear. This happened to me in the following story.

We were off duty in a tavern, and noticed two men come in, but we did not pay too much attention, as we knew one of them. They circled around behind us and left after having a few minutes of conversation. We found out later that the other individual had pulled an armed robbery and that he knew that we were on the robbery squad. He wanted to shoot us in the back, because he figured we were looking for him anyway, at least this is what our informant told us.

Sometimes informants make up information just to get on the good side of you, and we figured that this was the case here, because we knew that someone wouldn't be doing this while inside of a tavern, with witnesses around. It solved a robbery, because we later arrested this man by showing his photo to the victim, due to the information we obtained from the informant. Naturally, we could not admit to the fact that we knew what went down without telling on him, because it could have cost him his life.

So, you see, even though you are off duty you can get involved in life-threatening situations.

How would you feel if someone stated to you that you and your partner are to be killed and even told the day this would be carried out? Well, this happened! Check out the next chapter for details.

Chapter Fifteen
On an Assassination List!

An assassination list came to the attention of the chief of detectives and we were on it!

Naturally, upon receiving this information we were disturbed! They even named the date and who was going to kill us. Listen to this story!

There are some organizations which may or may not have a just cause for working in a community, and they may do some good, but then there are a few members who tend to overreact, which happened to be the case in our dealings with a radical organization here in Buffalo. They sprung up in an attempt to lure people to their side of thinking by hosting breakfast programs and other political benefits to further their cause, but the people living here did not fall for their particular brand of thinking.

To Be Killed

Joe and I became involved with them in the following manner. It wasn't that we were mistreating any of the persons on the East Side of the city of Buffalo, but someone had told them that we were arresting too many of the brothers. Here we were busting these individuals for armed robberies and all sorts of other crimes against their own people, for which the average person appreciated our assistance.

A police officer had reliable information that our assassination was to take place on June 1st, and in addition this organization was supposed to carry it out. (They even spelled my name right!) This was in a letter written to the chief of detectives, dated May 28, 1969. Information was forwarded that they were to start a riot in the city, to make Buffalo have as much trouble as the disorders in Chicago.

Waiting for the Bullet!

I have to tell you that I drove with my gun on the seat while in my own car. I even had it with me when I took out the garbage. This was mainly as a safety measure in the event they should try to try this assassination at my home or in my car. The chief of detectives asked us to take off that day, but we were not going to give in to any threats, so we worked anyway. We took care of the situation by driving to their headquarters and parking our car near the front door, thereby taking them by surprise, simply because there were just the two of us!

Naturally we had backup close by in the event they started shooting at us.

We were aware that they reinforced their building by putting cinder blocks out in front of the main part of the sidewalk, in the event of an attack by the police or anyone else. We called over to the guards who were in front of the property. One of them came over to the car and made the mistake of sticking his head in our window saying, "What the hell do you guys want?" He then noticed that I had a shotgun pointed directly under his chin, while his head was still inside of our car window.

"We heard that you were looking for us and wanted to kill us," I said. When he asked who we were, we answered, "Schwartz and Chernetsky. We're just paying a visit."

"You must be mistaken; we never intended to kill anyone!" was his reply as he gasped because of the shotgun under his chin. Apparently, they decided to leave town, not because of us, but because people weren't buying their program.

There were other occasions when certain officers were to be killed. There is a sense of humor on the department and is not meant to be cruel. There was word about a possible hit on one of the men on a particular squad. A jokester put up a sign which said: "This way to so and so's desk." The sign was a large bull's-eye, with an arrow pointed towards the officer's desk.

I remember when another detective was to be hit. No one wanted to ride with him, saying, "They may get me mixed up with you."

So ends the threats that a lot of police officers are sometimes confronted with while in the performance of their duties. Some are verbal and some are written.

How would you feel if someone wanted to kill you and it was brought to your attention by a reliable source? What would your response be?

Now you have all these stories about off-duty occurrences in your head. Is it what you thought it would be?

In the next chapter I wrote a poem about the feelings of working policemen when they do their job.

Chapter Sixteen
Poem

I wrote a poem about my feelings about the job, for a philosophy course, written in December 1978.

The Human Animal!

Feel the darkness of the streets at night
As the Sun is at rest.
Humans try to stay in their nest.
But out comes the animal and its fright.
Some animals hover and stare.
While others look and wait
One such animal struck his mate.
As they gaze and are aware
The human animal is now loose
He prowls the streets seeking prey,
Thus keeping others at bay
His attempt is to seduce
A probable victim to be
Where can one hide from the fright?
In the darkness of the night?
As they attempt to flee
To run away
Where to escape
To hold this animal at bay
To seek a safer place.
To hold this animal at bay.

A life as a cop, throws you into this abyss!
Hide all this in your head; Stuff the beast way back there.
To bring them out, you do not dare!
You cannot escape from this.

This poem speaks for itself, perhaps explaining the frustrations that policemen, firemen and rescue workers go through as they deal with the ordeals of situations confronting them on a daily basis. Sometimes you can't let go of what you have seen, heard, smelled, or touched while on this job, because it stays in your head, and this is why cops go to cop bars, and talk the talk, because they can't take this home with them. These feelings sometimes stay with you your whole life.

* * *

In the next chapter, follow along as precinct detectives are thrown into the lives of various people which they are called upon to assist.

Chapter Seventeen
Precinct Detectives

Do you ever wonder how detectives work their caseload? Or what goes through a detective's mind when confronted with episodes of people's lives? When you enter into their lives, you don't know if you can help them with their particular state of affairs, and in addition, if you do, maybe they won't like your idea of a quick fix.

You realize they will have to stay where they are while you will return to your safe environment when you complete your investigation on whatever their particular complaint was that you may, or may not have handled to their satisfaction.

Back to Square One!

In 1978, the police department went back to the precinct concept, causing it to be the first change in 16 years, as budget cutbacks and a reduction in manpower forced the commissioner to end what was known as the detective districts.

I was transferred from the robbery squad and went to Precinct No.5, located on the west side of the city. I looked forward to the challenge, which was working on all aspects of criminal investigations, because all I worked on previously were armed robberies while on the robbery squad.

Shuffling Papers

The first thing you do when you come into the office is to look through your caseload. Then you sort them in the order of priority, in this manner putting the most serious cases first, and in addition to this you have to answer calls on the streets.

Actually you are shuffling people's lives, which are carried in your paperwork.

Here are some of the cases which I investigated under the precinct detective concept.

* * *

I answered a call of a woman stabbed, and upon arrival on the scene, I found an 81-year-old woman on the floor with a huge butcher knife stuck in her back. While looking at the knife protruding from her back, we could see that there was no blood at this time, but we dare not pull it out for fear of causing more harm, due to the fact that she would then bleed to death.

It was while we were awaiting the arrival of an ambulance that I lay down next to her and while holding her hand, she whispered, "It was one of my tenants. He needed the money, and when I refused to give it to him, he stabbed me. He lives in the building next door."

When the ambulance came, I left her and immediately went to the suspect's home and up the stairs. I found him calmly eating dinner with his family. I grabbed him out of his chair, and while so doing, he had the nerve to say, "She bent my knife." At this moment I dragged him over to a side door, which opened to a fire escape, and I noticed that I was being filmed by a TV crew. Persons told me I had this strange look on my face as I came out the door. "What were you thinking?" one officer asked me. "You don't want to know," was my response. I then took him downstairs to the squad car and drove back to the station house to book him.

* * *

This next case involves the abuse of teenage girls. A woman loved her boyfriend so much, that she didn't want to believe that he was molesting her girls, even though the court took them away from her previously, because of prior molestations.

At this particular time, she wanted the girls home for the holidays, but he molested the girls again, and the mother still didn't believe them.

The courts ordered us to meet the social workers in front of the house, so that we could assist them in removing the girls from this atmosphere. The woman was in tears and yelled to her neighbors, "They are taking my girls." The neighbors were upset, because they didn't know what was going on, and they started screaming at us. "Leave those girls alone," while we were trying to place the girls into the police car. "Let them be with their mother," they screamed, over and over. The girls were turned over to the social service department. He was arrested again, with the mother shaking her head in disbelief.

* * *

Six-Year-Old Girl Abused!

"It was dark outside; she was naked, tears streamed down her face, when she tried to find her way home. She knew that she lived near the railroad tracks, and she also knew that she could see the church steeple, which was near her house, and then she will go home and tell her mother that some bad man had taken her away and hurt her."

I found myself investigating this abduction. After briefly speaking with the girl in the presence of her parents I immediately called for the policewoman to help in questioning her because there was a possibility of a sexual assault. The explanation she gave was unclear, but she did remember that he had worn a jacket, like her daddy had, with an automotive emblem on the outside. There wasn't much else for us to go on at this time, because all the little girl could tell us is that he was a white man with blond hair.

We did a foot canvass of the neighborhood and came up with a witness. She said, "I saw a strange boy chasing my kids. I went outside to see what was going on, and he took off." She later remembered that she saw him with the little girl, but didn't think anything of it, as he appeared to be playing tag with her in her own backyard.

We talked to a crossing guard and gave her his description. We spoke with her again the next day. She said, "Some of the children had complained about a boy bothering them, with a first name of Mark."

The little girl did recall hearing someone calling to the man who took her, and saying, "Mark." This must have occurred when the boy's mother called to him to come home for supper. At the same time he must have hidden her in the cardboard box in the field, but he did not leave her.

The name struck a bell! I remembered that we had a bike theft that I had investigated earlier in which a juvenile by that name was involved. I checked our files and found his full name and address. I went over to where he lived and spoke with his aunt. I asked her for permission to take his jacket, which fit the description given to us by the little girl.

We were unable to acquire a picture of him from our local schools, as he came from Rochester, New York, but we managed to obtain a high school photo from his home with the permission of his aunt, to show to our victim.

After first getting an identification of the jacket, we then showed her this picture, mixed in with similar high school pictures, and while in the presence of her mom and dad. She identified the picture as being the same man who took her away with him and hid her in a cardboard box in a field.

We found out that the boy was in detention on another matter, and we received permission from his father and the detention officials to question him. It was learned that he had permission to leave the premises occasionally on weekends. The young man admitted that he had a jacket like she had described. He mentioned he wore it on that particular day but would not admit to being near her house.

We then filed a petition in family court against him, on the molestation of the little girl. A judge qualified her in court, which is the procedure to establish whether the child is able to understand the truth.

There had been three court adjournments, which upset the victim's father, because this boy had been going by their house several times and was looking in their backyard. The father remarked, "I was afraid to go near him, because of what I might do to the him physically." This unpleasant incident caused the family to become upset with the court system, thereby refusing to let her return. This resulted in the dropping of the charges. The judge ordered him to stay away from the area of her house.

The court system failed her and her family.

* * *

Harassment by Phone

There was one incident in which this person avoided capture, and then he would call our station house to harass us, because he figured that we would not be able to discover where the call was coming from. We had a hunch one day while he was on the phone threatening us, as he usually had been in the habit of doing. We sent a squad to his house with a portable radio.

They sneaked up on the porch and rang his doorbell, while he still was on the telephone.

We knew from past experiences just what his doorbell sounded like, because it had an unusual ring to it. We told our men this fact through their portable radio. Our man told us, "I have to go for a minute to answer the door." We could hear the unusual ring to it. When he did, our men got him, which then enabled our squad to go on the phone and confirmed the fact that he was connected to our station.

They made him apologize to us on the same phone he had used to intimidate us. In the end he was trapped by his own phone which he had used to harass us.

We could never figure out whey he didn't just hang up when he went to answer the door!

Listen to this experience in which we captured a suspect in an unusual way.

Just Honk the Horn!

We arrested this person, and while at headquarters, he said, "I want to call my brother to let the family know what happened!" It was at that time that we remembered that this man's brother was also wanted. My partner, Detective Tony Constantino, took the phone, and during the course of his conversation, asked him where he was.[14] The man stated that he was at home, and then remarked to Tony, "Look, I don't want a police car parked in front of my house, and I don't want any police officer in there looking for me scaring my family. Just honk the horn as if you were just picking me up for a ride."

We agreed to do this, and upon our arrival at his house, we tooted the horn! He walked out of the house and into our car, thereby surrendering to us on our warrant.

The newspapers then wrote up this story and it appeared in the paper with the caption, "Honk brings suspect into police hands," in so doing explaining the particulars of what led up to this surrender.

* * *

In this next story a boy is thrilled to take a ride in an ambulance, but he is molested

He was only six years old, when an ambulance driver offered to give him a ride in the ambulance, but the man ended up molesting him. The child didn't tell his parents about this until some two weeks later. The ambulance service was located near the boy's house.

We found out where our suspect lived, which was in the suburbs, and asked the police from that location to watch our suspect's house while we obtained a warrant. We arrived just in time, as he was backing out of the driveway with his suitcases packed because he was about to leave town. He was put under arrest.

We were in the process of driving him back to Buffalo, when he looked at the car door. The thought entered our mind that he may try to jump out. Someone always sits in the back seat with the prisoner, because you don't want him behind the driver's seat, in the event he should attack the driver. It can be fatal!

Get this, never mind what happened to the child who was molested, his attorney wanted to make sure that his client was treated with the best of care by any police officer who may have come in contact with him. Read on!

We arrived back in our office when the desk officer told us that the man's attorney called and said, "Get the name of the officer at the desk! Get the name of the officer at our current stop! Get the physical condition of his client!"

The same thing happened before!

After he was the taken into custody, he spoke to his attorney on the phone, in our presence. "They got me for the same thing that I did in Houston." He told us that he served five years probation on this which was only two and one half years ago.

My partner and I received a letter of commendation in our file, from the parents of the boy who wrote the commissioner a very nice letter. They stated they respected the way we handled this case and appreciated the fact that we arrested this man for what he did to their boy. I was with a detective named John at that time, and I had the privilege of working with his father who was on the police department as well.[15]

* * *

Why Did They Hire Him?

A local hospital in Buffalo hired a doctor without even checking out his credentials. Local newspapers said that it boggles the mind that several colleagues of a Massachusetts doctor failed to mention his recent conviction for rape, in their writing of letters of recommendation, in order for him to get a job here in Buffalo.

This hospital had hired him without checking him out. If they would have bothered to run a background check they would have discovered that there were charges in the state of Massachusetts for molesting other patients, as well as a nurse.

Alerted by their authorities, we started a search for the doctor at his last known address. We staked it out for hours, only to find out later that he had escaped with the help of some of his friends.

He hired an attorney, and turned himself in to the authorities, so that he wouldn't be embarrassed. However his picture ended up in the local newspaper, along with a detailed story about what he did, and the fact he had references, never checked out by the hospital here in Buffalo.

* * *

Sometimes the effort to apprehend someone can be complicated as in the next case.

Two Willies

We were looking for this man on a warrant and spent two months trying to find him. We received a tip from an informant that he could be back in jail.

This was the first place we checked when we first started looking for him but as it happened he had gone to jail at a later date. We checked the jail again, and the deputy said, "Yep, we have two identical Willies with the same last name, and the same date of birth."

"Do a comparison fingerprint check on both of them," I asked. Sure enough, it ended up that one of the Willies was ours. The local newspaper had written this up as, "A case of the Willies," and stated that "he robbed and assaulted two Buffalo women. Sgt. Chernetsky laid the additional charges following an investigation."

* * *

In the next case the assailant got so greedy for money he didn't care what he did to his victim.

Tore Her Thumb Off!

In this particular crime this mugger tried to snatch a woman's purse. She would not let go of it, because the strap was bound on her hand and wrapped around her thumb. He then continued dragging her, and wouldn't give up, thereby yanking so hard that he pulled her thumb out of its socket. He then took off running down the street.

A description in the local papers said, "Man arrested, who tore the thumb off of a fifty-eight-year-old woman during a purse snatch." We came about this arrest because of the fact he was bragging to his friends about how he did this crime.

* * *

The following story is unusual as it pertains to a family matter and ended up with the hostage negotiating team being called out.

Hostage

A desperate father took hostage his 14-month-old son. It must be noted that when officers answered the call, he was at the front door with a gun to the infant's head while he was talking to them. He later let go two of his other hostages but kept the baby boy. It was during this confusion, upon the release of the hostages, that he managed to escape out a side door without anyone seeing him.

In the days that followed, my partner and I negotiated with his family, and made arrangements to have the baby turned over to his sister. We met with her in a supermarket parking lot. We took the boy and handed him over to Erie County child protection agency. Our picture was taken by the local media, upon the release of the child to the relatives. It was a big story at that time!

It was because of our negotiations that an agreement was set up for the father to turn himself in to his minister. It was under eerie circumstances.

Can you believe that it happened on Good Friday, at about twelve noon, at the Calvary Baptist Church, when we made the capture along with other detectives? We searched him inside the church, which upset his attorney, and the reverend there, because we figured he might be armed, and wanted a shootout to leave this earth in a blaze of glory. However he came peacefully.

* * *

In this next episode we had to con a criminal into reporting a crime.

His car had numerous bullet holes in it!

In this particular case, a man did not want to report the damage done to his car, because he leased it. This was after an Uzi (Israeli machine gun) shot up his vehicle as certain individuals were trying to kill him when he tried to flee from them.

We wanted to make sure that we had a crime report, relative to the gang activities. We asked him what he was going to tell the car dealer from whom he rented his vehicle. He didn't want to state that anything happened, nor would he say who did this to him. But after some thought he changed his mind and reported that some men tried to kill him, and he drove away at high speeds, while his car was being riddled with machine-gun fire.

Our purpose really was to have this report that he was engaged in some type of guerrilla warfare with his rivals, so that we would have a record on paper, because of his activities during his drug dealings with these particular individuals.

* * *

In an earlier report "Shots were fired," on this same spot a few days earlier, in which we investigated.

We managed to obtain a description from a man who was up on a telephone pole doing repairs, and he told the story in this way. "I was doing my job up here, when I noticed this man running across the lawn, and then two cars came from opposite directions and they had their windows rolled down and were firing at him. He returned fire, half-running, half-stumbling, and disappeared into that apartment."

We checked out the neighborhood and went into the apartment the telephone man said. The occupants of the apartment indicated that they didn't hear any shots. I then pointed to their door, and said to them, "How then do you account for all the bullet holes in your door, if you didn't hear anything?"

"We heard nothing at all!" was their reply!

Just Like TV

We located an elderly woman, who happened to be looking out the window and saw this same incident. She said, "It was like watching one of the police shows on TV. I saw the whole thing go down. The man involved in the gunfight is the same man who entered that apartment." She then pointed in that direction, and it was the same apartment where we noticed the bullet holes.

There was even another report filed, that during other gang activities that someone threw a hand grenade from a car while engaged in drug-related crimes.

I guess it would have made a good TV story!

* * *

In this next occurrence you would think that you would be safe just going out to lunch.

And while on the subject of gunfire, I want to mention at this time that I was working in a high-crime-rate precinct, and didn't want to tie up a police car to go out for lunch, so I had permission to use my own private vehicle.

I was just coming back from lunch, and was about to pull into the driveway of the precinct house, when I noticed a woman in the street, and she was about to fire a handgun in my direction. I was forced to dive from my car, roll in the street, and pull out my revolver, while turning my attention to her, thinking I might have to shoot her.

It seems that she was after this man who had decided to seek the safety of the precinct house. He was running for the front door at the same time I was coming into the driveway.

Pow!

Pow!

She fired five shots at him before she dropped her gun in the street as various police officers came outside to see what was going on. There were no bullets in my car nor in me!

We found out that she had bought the gun on a corner that is noted for drug dealers. She told us "I paid 30 dollars for the gun and five dollars apiece for each bullet. I don't remember who I bought it from."

I was thinking about what the evaluation would be if I would have shot her.

* * *

How would you feel if you went to a house looking for someone and expected to speak with him and then find out that he had passed on? A headline in our local newspaper told the story this way: "Deceased victim subpoenaed too late.

They Subpoenaed a Dead Man

Sometimes you have to have compassion for people and you have to reach out to them! I picked up this man in my own car to take him to court. He had the courage to face up to an attacker even though he was an elderly man and put himself on the line for doing this. I learned that he was subpoenaed to appear in court on a certain day in March, and went to his home to pick him up and it was at that time that his wife told me that

"Didn't you know? He died on January 30th."

I wonder if you can imagine how I felt at this particular moment when she informed me that he was dead, and when he passed on.

The signing of the subpoena raised some questions, in that someone had made a mistake, leaving the district attorney's office to state that there must have been a mixup in the paperwork. I explained his absence to the judge. "The man is dead, Your Honor! And he died on January 30th, but according to our court records he was subpoenaed in March." This announcement left the judge looking as confused as I was. Someone just dumped it in the mailbox and signed that they had served it on him personally.

* * *

In this next case you would think that if you let your children out just to go to a dance that they would be safe.

Are Your Kids Safe at a Dance?

This appears to be a simple question but on this particular night, there was a Christmas Eve dance in a local nightclub in the heart of downtown Buffalo. There was a disturbance inside the bar, and the bouncers ordered the two men who were involved in the fracas to go outside. They failed to obtain their names, because they just wanted them to leave the premises so the club they worked for would not be accountable. They took the easy way out!

The dance was just breaking up, and one of the two men who were involved in the fight earlier had returned, pulling up in a car and spraying the parking lot with machine-gun fire with an Uzi (Israeli machine gun).

It was a miracle that persons were only grazed, because the parking area was small. The victims wouldn't, or couldn't contribute any information on the shooter or on his car, stating that it was dark outside and that they were too busy ducking for cover.

The parents were just happy their kids survived this ordeal, but they were unable to get them to come up with any additional information, and were also grateful that we cared enough to try to keep the investigation going.

The bouncers didn't know who the persons they ejected were, because, as I stated previously, no one bothered to get their names.

The public probably doesn't know this, but some good street officers and detectives get the names of persons they talk to, and write it down, maybe not necessarily in their presence. Because if you were just thrown out of this club, after giving out your real name, would you even consider coming back and doing anything criminal in that area? Think of the above case. If the bouncers would have obtained the identification of these individuals we would have had names to go on.

Years later, after I retired, there was a lawsuit against the club owners!

* * *

A Friend of Mine Is Shot in the Chest!

A detective friend of mine, Mike O'Connor, answered a "man with a gun" call at a barber shop! He questioned the barber and was told that he had seen this man with a gun, and that the man was now walking down the street, thereby pointing to him! Mike yelled to him, "Stop!" It was at this moment the person then turned around towards him, and shot Mike in the chest. Despite his wounds Mike wrestled him to the ground.[16]

An FBI agent, who happened to be driving by, stopped his vehicle and saved Mike. He applied a tourniquet to the wound. It was later determined that the man who shot him thought Mike wanted to question him about the two murders he did the night before. *Did you get this? He just admitted he killed two people!*

In an additional story, Mike was working another job while off duty and arrested a shoplifting suspect. When he called for a warrant check on that person, unfortunately in his presence, it was at this time that this individual managed to disarm him while he was talking on the phone.

This person then ended up killed in a gunfight in Cleveland, Ohio, and it was found that he had Mike's gun on him when he died.

* * *

A call can have some twists and turns as we found out when we answered this bank alarm.

I responded to a call of a bank robbery, and was the first car on the scene. I had enough sense to wait for backup because I was in plainclothes, and it was the procedure. I did not want another police officer to shoot me, who did not know who I was, since I had a gun in my hand, even though I had my badge pinned to my lapel.

My backups came and gave me the nod. I entered the bank through an entrance which had a slight curve in it, but I could still see the teller with both his hands straight up in the air. I noticed that the teller was gesturing with his hand, over to his right, which was my left, and I looked in that direction and spotted a man standing in front of the teller's cage.

I then pointed my gun at him and forced him to the floor while I held him there, but I didn't see any weapon in his hand or on him when I searched him, along with the other officers.

We found out that there was no robbery in progress, just an irate customer. The teller was chewed out for using the holdup alarm and overreacting with his hands held high in the air.

* * *

Riding Alone!

Would you believe that at this time, in the year 2004, that Buffalo police officers ride alone, due to a new ruling by the mayor, on a contract the police union was forced to adapt, but with a promise of a certain sum of money. And as of this writing (2007), they still didn't get the money promised to them and are in the process of taking court action against the city.

My personal opinion on riding alone is if something serious were to go down, at the least you would have a witness to any action you might take. A suspect might shoot one officer, but would be a little leery about shooting it out with two officers, thinking that the other officer would surely kill him in the exchange of gunfire.

* * *

Hurt on the Job!

How is this for a day's work?

An injured-on-duty report was filed with the department, which stated as follows: "When apprehending several suspects, Sgt. Chernetsky was struck above the right eye with a sharp object, knocked down a flight of stairs, tore the banister off the wall, which slowed down his speed, hit the bottom of the stairs, and slammed into the opposite wall thereby striking his head."

A caption in the local paper indicted that "Sgt. Chernetsky was treated in a hospital for a facial laceration and sprained finger of his right hand and subsequently was released but he remained on duty."

I said to myself on that particular day, I must have nine lives and wondered how many I may have left!

* * *

In this next series of events there were an unusual number of arrests made when we worked a normal tour of duty.

Going My Way!

We received an excellent write-up in the paper due to the amount of arrests that we made during a ride downtown to book a few prisoners. The heading in the paper read: "Genesee Station Detectives were kept busy on Thursday arresting, six suspects in four separate incidents within five hours."

In the first such incident, we assisted in the capture of three burglary suspects, while searching the house after a K-9 officer had answered the original call. After booking these three men, we were on the way back to the station house.

In the second incident, we spotted an individual wanted by us on a warrant and we arrested him.

We tried to get back to the station house again.

In the third incident, we saw a man breaking into a van, who was trying to steal about one thousand dollars' worth of video equipment. We caught him red handed and booked him.

In the fourth incident, we decided to check out a group of suspicious men. A call was made to radio for a warrant check, and it disclosed that one of them was wanted.

We arrived at the precinct after booking this last man and didn't venture out on the street again and thought about how lucky we were.

How many times can you get that fortunate, to come upon all these arrests, not only in this one tour of duty, but one arrest after another before we could get back to the station house again.

* * *

In the following case, the victim's father didn't know that he was on camera while administering some street justice. The next story explains the events leading up to this TV news story!

We were investigating a burglary that ended up being a kidnapping, because the burglar took a young girl from the apartment. A check of the crime scene disclosed that he left an empty wine bottle and a hat on the scene. These articles were then sent to the police lab for analysis.

A news crews happened to come upon a mob scene, whose actions were directly involved in this particular case.

Smile, You're on *Candid Camera*

A news camera crew filmed a mob punching and kicking a suspect, while the father of the victim was stabbing him while in the process of administering some street justice.

The father of the victim was placed under arrest due to his appearance on TV. This left no room for doubt, as the DA's office and the police had no choice in this matter.

The district attorney's office dropped the charges against the father after further review of the circumstances involved. The girl was later found unharmed, but went to the hospital anyway where she looked at a series of mug shots, in which she positively identified our suspect as the man who kidnapped her.[17]

Saving Lives

There are times when you save someone's life and they don't even thank you, but chalk it up as a daily occurrence of life on the dirty side of the world.

This has been repeated in other incidents where life and death is just a roll of the dice.

Two More Lives Saved

We were patrolling a high-crime area of the city. We rounded this corner and spotted a man who was about to shoot two youths that he had up against a wall. We confronted him and ordered him to drop the shotgun, or we would shoot him! He complied with our request and said, "I was going to shoot them because of a prior fight down the street."

Here is another example, of saving people's lives, because if we had not come around the corner as we did, he would have killed them with a blast from his shotgun.

* * *

About to Be Stabbed

In a similar incident, we came upon a call of a disturbance in a parking lot. We leaped out of the car just in time to see two men who had this woman down on her back, and one of them was about to plunge a knife into her chest. His arm was raised above his head, ready to strike. But he heard my shout, and noticed the barrel of my gun, a 9mm Glock, which looked to him like the Grand Canyon, so I knew what his response would be, when I yelled, "Stop or I'll shoot." The blade stopped in midair as he dropped his knife and stood up with his hands raised over his head. It was over!

The woman then said to us, "I don't want to press charges," even though it appeared that this man was going to kill her, and that we saved her life. She figured that if she were to pursue this matter, and prefer charges against them, that she would be signing her death warrant!

We arrested the men on disorderly conduct and weapon charges.

Now, again, I will ask you the reader, to tell me what you think that the powers to be, who might be judging this case, perhaps months later, would rule if I had killed him. Or, if I was riding alone and had no witness to this occurrence.

* * *

Here is another event when you think you are just doing a routine thing, by just serving some paper when you find yourself in a situation.

I was alone and in the process of just serving a summons, when I spotted an individual who was wanted. It was my case to investigate as I had prior knowledge that he had fired five rounds from a handgun at three females and one male in an earlier occurrence, and there was an impending warrant.

I pretended to be just interested in his car, and I tried to make it appear that I was calling for a plate check, when in reality I was calling for backup.

I managed to maintain a grip on him as he was standing outside his vehicle, at the same time telling him he was under arrest. I attempted to put him spread eagle against his vehicle, but because of snow and ice on the street, he managed to spin around, to push me, to reach into his pocket, while facing me. This led me to believe that perhaps he may be going for a gun, because of his past case history. I could have shot him, but instead I fired one shot in the air and warned him to freeze as I pointed my weapon directly at him. He threw off his coat, while an unidentified female took it from the ground and ran into the house with it. At this time, the suspect was running away from me, and was yelling on the top of his lungs, "Shoot me, Shoot me!"

I fired two more warning shots into the dirt

Pow!

Pow!

which was by an empty field, across from his house.

The suspect now had doubled back at this time, while the female let out their great Dane dog. This move added more confusion to the matter! Here I'm chasing this person down the street, and here was this great Dane running alongside of me, barking at me, as if it was some kind of game, but the dog made no attempt to bite me.

Can you picture this?

Officers of the TPU (tactical patrol unit) finally captured the suspect as he tried to round the corner thereby cutting him off with their patrol car.

When he was testifying in court, he said, "The detective tried to kill me! He fired at me, but he was a poor shot and missed me."

I confronted him outside the courtroom and said to him, "If I wanted to kill you I wouldn't have missed and surely would not be firing warning shots in the air and into the dirt."

We obtained a warrant for the female for filing a false crime report on another matter, but in this case, we couldn't prove that the gun was in the coat when she ran into the house with it. However, I must add a sad note, because some years later, there was a drive-by shooting in which this same woman ended up sprayed with machine-gun fire, thereby leaving her crippled for life.

Sometime after this, someone shot a police lieutenant with an assault rifle at the same spot, but he survived because the bullet just grazed his shoulder. We investigated this along with the homicide squad and could not come up with anything, although we spent several months on it.

It could have been the fact that the shooting was at night, and no one in the neighborhood would assist us relative to this matter, or maybe they were afraid to do so, for their lives were at stake.

* * *

The next story is about a poor old lady who came into the station house to report an accident.

Fender Bender!

An elderly woman came into the station house and quickly approached the front desk. She tried to get the attention of the desk officer.

I was up front with the day lieutenant and heard her say to the desk officer on duty, "I want to report an accident." The officer at the desk was prepared to make out the paperwork, and asked her questions about the accident.

"I am supposed to meet a certain patrol officer here at the stationhouse," she said, and then went on to say. "This accident is with one of your police cars." She then handed the desk officer a piece of paper on which she indicated that the officer with whom she had the accident had written his name. Both of us studied the name and it was not familiar to us. She added that the officer had struck her car broadside and then after getting out of his patrol car, he asked her to meet him here. We asked her what he looked like, and she described him and the uniform he was wearing. This sounded like one of our officers all right. However, we still had our doubts about this, until she reached down, and pulled up a piece of the fender, in so doing placing it on the counter for us to look at.

I must mention that the fender could not be seen from our view, when she was up front talking to the desk officer, as it was down below our line of vision when she was standing at the desk.

It was unbelievable, as we looked at the fender on the counter, and then realized that she had in fact obtained a fender from one of our police vehicles. "My sister is still stuck in the car," she blurted out.

We immediately went outside, to the station house parking lot, and discovered her sister still strapped in the car. The car was dented at the door, and her sister was trapped against it. We tried to release the seat belt, but without success, and ended up cutting the strap with a knife. We summoned an ambulance for her, and they responded quickly, but closer examination determined that she was not injured.

Further inquiry disclosed that she did have an accident with a marked police car, and that the police officer left the scene of the accident and never called an ambulance for her sister. Although he had given her a fictitious name and took off from the scene of the accident, we were still able to track him down through a radio broadcast on the damage to his car. We were surprised to hear over the radio "You, in police car number 65, pull your car over, pull over now," as a certain captain used the police radio to bark out this command. It ended up that the officer in question was a rookie, scared, and out of his area when he hit the ladies' car, and was trying to cover his ass by this particular deception. Of course the department held a hearing on his actions with regard to this serious matter, and he was reprimanded for his lack of action relative to this particular accident.

* * *

This case was strictly for the birds.

Someone took a costly mynah bird worth $2,000-plus during the course of a burglary in an only-one-of-its kind situation. We received a tip on where the bird could be and went to that address to check it out. We wanted to see if there was any merit to this information. The burglar in question had an elaborate alarm system of his own set up, which consisted of TV cameras. We peeked in the window and noticed there was a bird inside, just sitting on a perch. We then managed to get the owner to come and look, and she said, "Sure looks like my bird, all right!"

It was at this time we obtained a search warrant and returned to that same address thereby executing the warrant, even though no one was home at the time, which was legal according to the terms of the warrant. After receiving no response to our knocking at the door, we then elected to kick in the door to gain entry!

We got to the bird, and tried to get it into a box which we had brought with us. But we were unable to do so, as we had a hard time trying to make sure the bird was not harmed in the process. (we had no cage). The lieutenant yelled "Ouch" as he received bite marks on his finger and he was lucky he didn't lose it, as the bird gnawed a circle around it. I had to hit the bird with a judo chop gently on the back of the wings to get him into the box, leaving the bird unhurt after this experience. We returned it to his rightful owner.

We took a lot of verbal abuse from other officers, who thought that the whole incident was funny and they would then remark to us, "Ha, judo chopping a bird. Are you sure you guys could handle the situation? We could have provided backup for you if needed."

As I have indicated many times prior to this, you jump to the beat of the drummer, which is the police radio dispatcher! How many of you would do this job, especially if you put your life on the line every day, and hop into this frying pan again and again, for the salary the police get? The danger is always present, and even if you are in plainclothes and have a gun in your hand, another police officer could shoot you, especially if you are in an undercover capacity.

Someday you might be in a position to take a life, or seriously hurt someone for your own protection, or shoot someone for the protection of another person. Then someone in authority will take a few months to figure out if you did the right thing, concerning your split-second decision on the street. In the concrete jungle, as some officers will call the street, they will then say to one another upon greeting, "Be careful, it's a jungle out there!" The beat goes on in this line of work. It's not a thing that the average citizen has to concern himself with, only the officers who answer the calls and work the streets of any large American city, while walking this Thin Blue Line! There you have it. The detective case load which occurs on a daily basis. I must add at this time that the department went back to the detective districts concept shortly before I left the force in 1995! "Go figure!"

For those who have been on the job for a while they study and hope to move up the ranks in promotions. I have covered this in the next chapter.

Chapter Eighteen
Promotions

I was on a lieutenants list in 1962, but the list expired. At that time, even if you are next on the list you will have to wait another four years before you would be able to take another exam.

"Some deserved it!"

"Some didn't."

"Some were political!"

"Some weren't."

That's the way it worked.

In 1964, I received a promotion to the rank of detective.

At the end of the '90s you had to take an exam for consideration to be promoted to the rank of detective or detective sergeant, and to me this is a good idea because it doesn't have to be political.

Some of my promotions:

November 1964: Promoted to detective.

January 27, 1973: Promoted to detective sergeant.

I received a certificate from the Buffalo Police Department for an in-service investigators course. April 25, 1973. This was a two-week course in supervisory training.

I was elected vice president of the Detective and Detective Sergeant's association for two years in a row in 1975 and 1976 and declined to run the third year.

Because of budget cuts, I had to take a bust in rank from detective sergeant to detective for a short time, effective July 1, 1976, but was reinstated before a month was up. I didn't lose my seniority!

The newspapers wrote up this story: "Six policemen were repromoted to detective sergeant after their positions were reinstated."

What was disturbing was officers were turning in their badges and their guns during these layoffs causing some three hundred police officers to lose their jobs and become civilians.

I had the opportunity to serve as an assistant chief of detectives for the C and D districts, which took in some eight precincts. I also served as assistant chief of detectives out of the headquarters office for several tours of duty, which took command of the city as a whole.

We, the sergeants, didn't think that it was fair, nor was it worth the money to assume the position of this job, which consisted of a huge responsibility, as the lieutenants ended up out of this job due to the budget cuts.

There was a class action suit filed by the sergeants, and the city backed off on detailing sergeants to this job classification and went back to using the lieutenants again. Budget cuts happened again on June 18, 1981, and I was sweating being busted down in rank again, but it didn't happen.

In 1988, I went to a three-day survival training in Toronto, Canada, because they did not offer this course in Buffalo. I had to organize my schedule and went on my own time, in so doing, spending my money for the course and hotel expenses.

I am sure that other officers who were participating in this course were surprised to see an older detective going in for this type of training. It was a great experience, and I learned a lot, although I wish that more officers would attend these in-service training courses."

However, certificates were put into my police file consisting of Ontario Police Journal Certificates that I satisfactorily completed Street Survival 88 ons August 24-25, 1988, along with The Tactical Edge Seminar conducted by Calibre Press Inc. and on August 26, 1988, the Win seminar. Included in this was a home video cassette entitled *Surviving Edge Weapons* for in-service training, which was also by Calibre Press.

In the next chapter I will try to explore the feelings which go on when woman is raped.

Chapter Nineteen
Rape

Women will tell you that nothing is more sensitive than cases in which they are a victim of a rape, along with the trying ordeal which most victims of this hideous crime have to endure. Not only when they are of age, but also when it involves the rape of a young person, or of a retarded person who would be unable to give consent. They have a sex offense unit that handles this type of crime. But as indicated previously we are sometimes there first, but we try to be gentle and usually call the policewomen, as men don't usually question women in such a sensitive area. If there is no choice in the matter, then the officers who answer the call will try to get a description of the attacker out over the air as soon as possible, but he or she has be sensitive to the feelings of the rape victim when they question them about it.

* * *

Here are some of the cases which I encountered during investigation of this crime of rape.

We had a series of rapes in which the criminal's description given by the victim was a short man, only five foot three inches tall, and the victims stated that he looked like Mighty Mouse.

We found a suspect and had a lineup in the station house, in which the victim of this rape identified him as the man who attacked her. Another woman who had given our policewomen the same identical description as the first victim also identified him when he appeared in the courtroom. We thought that this was the end of this series of rapes but they continued with the same description.

So, we continued our investigation in this matter, trying to clear our man. However, much to our surprise we found another man, who was the twin of this first man, but no relation, who fit the same profile, along with the same size, who also looked like Mighty Mouse, followed by the fact that he was also a weight lifter, or body builder. In this case, we arrested the wrong man, but worked to solve the rapes, and to our credit, we managed to catch the right one. We were not afraid to admit there was a mistake made.

The local newspapers wrote the story up and gave credit to the man's wife for standing by him in his time of need, by stating, "Wife had faith that her husband would be cleared."

* * *

Earlier I spoke of the frightening ordeal some women go through. Follow this case on what horrified this particular woman. When she thought it was over, it wasn't. Sometimes a woman's life changes due to circumstances because of the results of a violent crime such as the victim in this particular rape case.

Here's what happened to her!

It was still daylight, at that time. People were just leaving their jobs and going to their cars. In this incident two men took a young woman at knifepoint from a downtown parking lot. She was then driven to a project and taken to the fifth floor, where they raped her repeatedly. Then they took her to the roof, and told her that they were going to throw her off. But for some reason they changed their mind and left her there. She managed to get down off the roof and went to one of the lower floors, thereby banging on some apartment doors, seeking assistance from any occupant who would open their door to her pleas for help. Someone called an ambulance for her, along with a call to the police to come to the scene of the crime.

Yet, shortly before that call went out, other officers entered the building on another matter. They saw these two individuals leave the apartment building complex. The officers recognized them but were unaware of what had just transpired relative to the woman on the roof. When they found out, they turned their names over to the detectives, who thanked them for a nice piece of work.

We picked up the investigation, and she positively identified the mug shots we showed her, on the lead the officers had given. But that was not the end of her troubles, as her fiancée could not handle this, and he then told her that he couldn't marry her because he felt he would not be able to forget the incident due to the fact that two men violated her! He called their marriage off.

I can still remember her name, face, and what happened to her life, because that's how much this experience touched me. I hope some day she reads this book and knows of my concern for her at that time.

Have you ever been in a riot or involved in one? Check out the following events about riots which occurred in the Buffalo area.

Chapter Twenty
Riots

Have you ever found yourself in the middle of a riot, and had no idea how you ended up there and what your response would be?

* * *

Allentown Riot

The Allentown Art Festival drew thousands of people from all over western New York and started as a peaceful event. It was on the last day when all hell broke loose. I found myself and others who were with me in a riot.

Bottles and rocks were thrown from the roofs of various apartment buildings. We joined in the effort to try to apprehend those who threw them but when we arrived on the roof, we found out that they had fled, finding refuge in some apartments by persons who opened their doors to them, thereby protecting them from being arrested. The smell of tear gas, bricks and bottles were in the air as we tried to quell this disturbance.

Families with women and children in tow tried to stay out of the way but ended up being in the middle of this melee as tear gas filled the air they breathed.

According to some press reports, the area was a battleground. Still other reports mentioned that an individual waving a Viet-cong flag ended up arrested while in the middle of this skirmish.

* * *

The East Side

In the late '60s, there were riots in the downtown Jefferson area as several hundred youths went on a rampage! According to press reports there were thirteen persons injured and fifteen arrested from inside one drug store they were looting. A warning shot was fired by a security guard in trying to ward off the looters.

The mayor urged the closing of liquor stores and gas stations, where some of the looters were filling up bottles with gasoline and using them against the police.

Negro leaders were trying to restore calm to the city, as the local paper indicated. I had my picture in the paper with some of these leaders, along with Tom Day, who was a football player for the Buffalo Bills.

* * *

Student Riots

There were nationwide student protests of the United States' involvement in Cambodia and the deaths of four Kent State University students in a confrontation with National Guardsmen.

In addition, student riots flared up again in May of 1970 at the University of Buffalo, as picture windows of Norton Hall had been smashed, furnishing removed and broken up in nearby roadways, to build barricades against the police. As a result of this, some other area campuses were closed, namely Buffalo State and Canisius colleges. Most classrooms were closed, but a few students took the chance to leave early with no academic penalty.

This caused the police commissioner to say that it was most unfortunate that a small minority that advocates violence and lawlessness has been able to deprive the majority of students of their constitutional rights.

It was May 8, 1970, and another riot broke out at UB in which students were involved. The caption in the local newspapers stated that "thirty-five police, 22 students, and a guard were hurt at UB riots (University of Buffalo). One hundred students were engaged in throwing rocks and bottles at the police. Huge bonfires were started by these students. Firefighters came under attack when they responded to fight these fires." Firefighters responding to alarms ended up delayed briefly by students attempting to block their entrance to the campus itself. "Town of Tonawanda Police and twenty-five deputy sheriffs tried to contain the rioters within the city limits" (a nearby suburb). Can you believe this, attacking the firemen!

In one incident, a brick thrown by a rioter hit my partner, Joe, on the head! He had a helmet on when this happened, or he would have had serious head injuries. We chased the person who threw it all the way off campus, to a restaurant on Main Street. He sat down and pretended he was a customer who had been sitting there all along. However, he sure was surprised when yanked off the stool and placed under arrest for the assault on Joe.

Throughout these same student riots, the detectives were ordered into uniform before they were sent to confront these demonstrators. It was at this time that my partner and I were in an unmarked blue station wagon, when about 200 protesters came off campus and blocked the intersection. They spotted us because of the uniforms, and we had to call for a backup, but not before one of them hurled an iron bus stop sign, which smashed our rear window, and slid behind the back of Joe's head.

Again, he would have received serious injury, had it not been for an extended shelf behind the driver's seat, thereby causing it to miss his head and hit the shelf instead. The mob tried to pull us from the car during this struggle, half in, and half out of the car, as Joe managed to fire his shotgun in air.

This scared them because of the sight and sound of the gun going off, and they backed off the attack on us.

We found out later that there was an injury of an officer, as his was leg broken while coming to our assistance during this particular encounter.

In this same occasion, the local papers stated that several hundred students seized Norton Union Hall, and another 150 were holding Hayes Hall, thereby surrounding the police who were in front. We came to their assistance and broke through the doors, from the rear of the building, and out the front doors to rescue the police trapped there. We were successful in our efforts.

The local press wrote a story on what had occurred here in front of Hayes Hall, and praised the police for their restraint in this two-and-one-half-hour standoff.

Students were protesting the Vietnam War, with a chant, "One, two, three, four, we don't want your f…war!" as they hurled stones and Molotov cocktails at the police. The headlines in local newspapers screamed with the words, "Students and police battle as violence grips UB" (University of Buffalo), as false calls for ambulances tied up the area, as students had started an $8,000 fire at the gym, and at the headquarters of the Air Force ROTC.

In Amherst (close to the city line) police battled with them as the students charged into the university plaza area (another suburb).

How do we kill them?

The outcome for this riot even reached the capital as undercover officers testified in Washington, D.C., that they had attended speeches in which the students learned methods for killing Buffalo policemen.

* * *

Follow along, in the next chapter, while I relate to you the job of being a robbery detective. I put a transfer in for this specialized squad and spent some 20 years investigating street robberies along with numerous bank robberies.

Chapter Twenty-One
Robbery Squad

I went to the robbery squad in December of 1965 because of a transfer I requested. The investigations we worked on were usually armed robberies and bank holdups. The local police were responsible for the bank robbery cases even though the FBI sent agents to the bank, but then it goes into federal court under a federal bank act.[18]

*   *   *

A Good Partner

Joe Schwartz broke me in as a robbery squad investigator. We worked together for some eight years until the precinct concept broke up our partnership. This was like being married to one another, because we thought the same way, did the same actions on the street, at the same time without even talking.

Refer back to the chapter on Joe's retirement party!

Answering the Calls

As I have indicated in the introduction these calls are glimpses into people's lives. The patrolmen answer the call, start the paperwork, but it is the detectives who are more directly involved in their lives.

It is hard to describe these stories as one event leads to another because this is a day-in, day-out occurrence, as I have stated previously, because you answer to the beat of the radio operator. You are in the frying pan, day in and day out, as you respond to these calls.

However, who of you will walk that line with them? Who of you will chase an armed man, or go into a dark alley, for the salary that police officers get? I think not! How would you feel? What do you think you would do?

So, here it is! Follow along as we answer various calls along the way. This chapter is rather long because I was on this particular squad for over 20 years, and naturally there was more action, more danger, more stress, because we were always trying to take armed felons into custody.

* * *

In this episode I will relate to you what can happen when you answer a holdup call and the surprising events which occurred.

Look Behind You

My partner and I started this day by answering a call of an armed robbery of a bowling alley and heard the description go out. A check of the license plate disclosed the address of the suspect. It was dark out, and we took a position near his house.

However, after we acquired a spot on this dark street, a car pulled up right behind us, and I said to my partner, "What if it's them, they are behind us?" They were! As they alighted from the car, we were able to look at the plate, and sure enough it was the right plate, and lucky for us, they didn't see us. We caught them off guard by getting them from behind as they were walking away. It's a good thing we did it this way because they were both armed!

* * *

Things should be calm in your office, you would think. Check this incident out as we were talking to a suspect.

Look Before You Leap

We were questioning a suspect in our office which is located on the third floor of the headquarters building, in the downtown area of the city. The suspect made a run for the window! I don't know if he realized that we were up on the third floor of the building when he made his run to escape, but I managed to leap in the air, and with the force of my body, knocked him away from the window like a pool shot. This left the cadet assigned to our office, looking on in complete astonishment.

Same Window Another Time

A similar incident occurred when I was passing under this same window, and this time I was on the street below, and heard this loud crash, and as I looked up, I was startled to see someone come crashing down. In this event a suspect had his hands cuffed behind his back and had leaped out the window, falling, falling, and landing facedown on the concrete below. Lucky for him he landed in a huge snow bank which broke his fall. He was confined to a hospital for several months.

Would you believe that several months later, this same individual pulled an armed robbery, and ended up shot at by a member of our squad?

* * *

Talk about an unusual series of events. You would never expect this to happen to you while in the performance of your duties

Pissed All Over Me

In this strange story, there was an 80-year-old woman who was in a wheelchair because she only had one leg. She had a boyfriend, who was 70 years old, who lived with her. It was later learned that a man had broken into her house and then beat both of them, so he could get some money to satisfy his drug habit.

We arrested the suspect after canvassing the neighborhood, and found him in a downtown hotel where he put up a fierce fight, in which my suit was ripped, my watch was broken!

It wouldn't be the first time my watch was broken, or my suit ripped, and it wouldn't be the last time, as police officers sometimes go through this when someone resists arrest.

I picked the 80-year-old victim up and drove her to the courtroom. I lifted her out of her wheelchair to put her on the courtroom seat. But when she saw the suspect, she shrieked, waved her cane in the air, screamed at him, and pissed all over me!

Now, my suit was wet, but it didn't bother me one bit, as I already had a bad day, with the suspect resisting arrest while fighting fiercely, and now being pissed on. It was all in a day's work. Can you believe I still remember all this and it occurred in the year 1967?

* * *

All did not go well for these two holdup men as the following story relates.

A Failed Robbery Attempt
In this occurrence two men tried to hold up a pharmacy, but failed because the owner ran to the rear of the store. He called for help after one of the holdup men said to him, "This is it, put all the money in here," as he held out a paper bag.

When the owner ran, the other holdup man yelled, "Stop or I'll shoot," but no shot was fired. The two men ran to a waiting car, with a third man at the wheel.

A witness managed to obtain the license plate number of their car, just at the time the holdup men sped away from the scene of the crime.

According to newspaper accounts, a K-9 dog sniffed out one suspect hidden in a house, when a tactical patrol unit officer spotted the car and the dog obtained the scent. The dog, "King," ignored the house the man went into, but sniffed his way to another house, where another suspect ended up arrested at gunpoint without a struggle.

My partner and I obtained leads from a nearby tavern and arrested the other man at gunpoint, leaving their best plans foiled.

* * *

You're trying to do your job but the public must be informed. I was in the process of examining a crime scene and noted

Blood All Over
A story in the local paper said: "Three thugs beat Broker, flee with $7,400." "He was beaten brutally," Detective Michael Chernetsky of the

Robbery Squad said. "He left a trail of blood all the way to his apartment." As a result, while investigating this crime, a reporter took my picture and printed it in the paper.

We're Booking Your Brother

In this case I received a call that there was a man being booked downstairs. He said he was my brother, while being booked on a disorderly conduct charge. I knew before I even thought of going downstairs to question this individual that it couldn't be my brother, Tom, because he lived in Atlanta, Georgia.

So, I listened to his story and then asked him, "Do you know me?"

He said "No."

"I'm Mike Chernetsky," I informed him.

You should have seen the look on his face! He then explained to me, "I tried this scam because I read your name in the paper on many occasions and thought it would be a good idea to do this, thinking it might get me off. Can't blame a man for trying."

* * *

In the next case we had to arrest several young men who not only held the place up but killed their victims.

Teenage Killers

According to newspaper descriptions of this crime, "Two Buffalo teenagers today faced charges, in separate courtrooms. They killed a pharmacist in a weekend robbery! This robbery was pulled the day after the death of another man they were accused of shooting in a recent delicatessen holdup.

"With regard to the pharmacist, Sgt. Chernetsky said, 'He was partially deaf, and apparently didn't hear the command issued by the robbers, and then one of them fired a shot, which struck him in the back of the head.'"

As I have indicated previously, the job is dangerous, and it is always present in your mind that you don't know if you will come home or not. I know that you are probably tired of me saying this and thinking to yourself, "Yeah, right!" Well, listen to the following story about what almost happened to two robbery squad detectives, who were also good friends of mine.

Which Detective Should I Kill?

Here is a case where the suspect would even kill a police officer if need be.

One of our cars answered a call of a man with a gun in a downtown gas station. As they entered the station they were able to take an armed man into custody. Now, speaking about what is on the mind of the victims, or the officers, how about listening to what was on the mind of this particular criminal who caused this call.

I want you to listen carefully, as I tell you the rest of the story. It will make your hair stand up because of what almost happened to these two detectives.

When questioned at length, the suspect told me what was going through his mind. "I didn't know which detective to shoot when they entered the gas station. Lucky for them that they split apart. I was going to kill the first detective but was afraid of being shot by his partner." *Can you believe this?*

This deterred him from doing so! Now, what would have happened if there was only one of them who confronted with this individual, which is a case in point, as Buffalo went back to one-man cars just recently to save the city money (in 2004).

Even more riveting was the fact that he confessed that he had killed a man while he was living in another state and buried his body so no one would know what he did. He gave us a signed confession to this and even indicated where the body was!

Sure enough, when we contacted the authorities there, we found out that what he had told us was the truth, because the victim was listed as missing and in addition, they found the body right where he said it was. This left our own two detectives breathing a sigh of relief when informed of this.[19]

* * *

In this event we were after this one holdup man and he appeared to draw a line in the sand as he said

"You Can't Touch Me Here "

We investigated a stabbing and beating of an elderly 70-year-old woman who was in the hospital. We questioned the suspect earlier, but couldn't arrest him until she got well enough to look at mug shots. When she was able to do so, she identified him.

We then obtained a warrant for his arrest and received a tip on where we might be able to find him. He was working in a Main Street restaurant. As we approached him he remarked, "You can't touch me in here. I am working!" He wouldn't come quietly, so we had to reach across the counter and forcibly arrest him, thereby dragging him out of the restaurant anyway.

* * *

Sometimes your work is noticed. My partner and I were fortunate enough to get an award for our work.

Officer of the Month

My partner, Joseph Schwartz, and I received an award from our police officer's organization. This award was for a robbery that happened on November 17, 1971. Joe and I had our pictures in the patrol officer's newspaper when we were both nominated by their organization to be officer of the month.

This article stated, "On November 17, 1971, at approximately 5:30 P.M. a holdup occurred at a liquor store, in the Black Rock section of Buffalo. Det. Sgt. Schwartz and Det. Chernetsky of the robbery squad, immediately responded to the scene, and obtained a description of the getaway car, and holdup men, putting it over the air for any cars in the area.

"A short time later, a Kenmore Police lieutenant located the holdup car and notified the Buffalo Police Department." (Kenmore is a suburb just outside of Buffalo.)

"The two robbery squad officers then went to the location of the getaway car, and under the command of an Asst. Chief, they began a door-to-door canvass of the area, searching for suspects.

"At one point, a neighbor told the officers that she had seen a man, who fit the description, enter a house next to hers. The officers immediately entered the house, and obtained permission to search the building. They located the suspect hiding in a closet under a pile of clothes and arrested him at gunpoint. This arrest solved eleven other holdups in recent weeks, an excellent bit of work, by two of Buffalo's fine police detectives."

It was an honor to receive this award by the Patrolman's Organization. We always had a good relationship with the uniformed personnel!

We cooperated with, and received some excellent information from officers of the patrol force. We also received a certificate from the patrol officer's organization, relative to this same case. Because we were partners frequently, one of the patrolman's newspapers showed a picture of us, with a caption, "Where ever there's Schwartz, there's Chernetsky (Look closely!) "

* * *

The department established what was known as

The Awards Board

I was the first plainclothesman put on the awards board. We met once a month and went through various police files to ascertain if there was anyone who was deserving of any outstanding merit for his or her police work. This would be above and beyond what was expected of them.

In another development by the awards committee: They sent me a letter of commendation, which stated that, "As a result of your actions beginning on 9-13-92 when you solved an assault involving gunfire in your precinct through hard work and perseverance." I want to mention that I was not on the awards board at that time.

While on the subject of awards I must mention that in addition a plaque was given to me by the Detective and Detective Sergeants Association near the end of 1992 for "Distinguished Dedication to Duty."

* * *

I was surprised when an award was given to me by the mayor of the city of Buffalo for saving the life of a gunshot victim, while off duty, as told in the following story which occurred at a local supermarket.

Saved a Life on Second Job

I was working security on a second job, and had just returned to a local supermarket after depositing money in a nearby bank. I told the man I was riding with (not a cop), "Sounds like gunshots." To which he replied, "Nah, sounds like firecrackers to me."

I entered the store, looked around, and didn't see anything. I looked outside and went over to another exit door where I spotted a man lying on the ground with two bullets in his chest. One of the wounds was bleeding badly, so I applied first aid to the wound to stop the bleeding and at the same time I had two citizens assist me in holding him down. One comforted him and the other helped in holding him steady while he was trashing about. One of them was an off-duty state trooper.

The man was conscious and told me the name of the man who shot him and where he lived. I informed the first police car on the scene.

Would you believe that the suspect in question called 911 himself and told the dispatcher who he was and said, "I just shot a man in front of the supermarket and I want to turn myself in!"

The shooting happened this way. Our cart boy overheard the whole conversation, while crouched behind the carts in front of the store, and told us the following story.

He said, "The guy pulled up to the store, and got out of the car, just as this man and woman were entering. I heard him speak to the man. 'I told you to stay away from my wife.' The guy just kept walking. The shooter then said, 'I'm going to shoot you,' and the victim replied with, 'Go ahead, shoot me. At this time the shooter warned him again, and the victim stuck out his chest and said to the shooter, 'Shoot me if you must.' The shooter then pumped two bullets into the victim's chest."

* * *

You always have to follow through on tips which may or may not be true as was indicated in the following story which occurred in a bank.

Wrong Tip

In this particular incident I was seated at the manager's desk in a bank because we received a tip of a possible holdup.

I had instructed the teller nearest me to stack some coins on her counter and then to knock them over if this person should come to her cage and pass her a note. About five minutes later, I heard the sound of the coins falling to the floor. A man came up to her cage, and she then knocked over the coins! I leaped from my position armed with my shotgun in hand.

I had secreted a shortened version of a shotgun underneath the desk I was seated at.

It was at this time that the man at the teller's cage fell to the floor in fright because he saw me with the shotgun! I confronted him while he lay on the floor.

The explanation was that when the teller saw this man approach her cage, she was so afraid that she accidentally knocked over the coins. *Oops!*

We apologized to the customer and explained everything to him, to which he said that he was okay with that but he left the bank in a hurry because of this unfortunate experience which had just happened to him.

We never did find out why this had not come down, as this was the information forwarded to us. But sometimes you get a bum tip and sometimes as I have indicated before, informants like to play you like a harp, trying to store up points.

* * *

We were pleased to see that a local paper praised our work in an article: "An intense period of 21 hours of continuous investigation, by two detectives, led to the arrest of a suspect for two recent armed robberies of gas stations. Detectives impounded a car he fled in, and searched a house he went into, where the suspect was found hiding in the attic."

In this particular case, I would like to say that the attic in question was pitch black, so black that when we went up the stairs we couldn't even see our hand in front of our face. I told my partner, "I can hear him breathing! Come out with your hands up," we shouted in the darkness. He did as we commanded and was unarmed! He had some of the loot from his recent holdup on him.

* * *

This individual in the following article has just returned from service in Vietnam when he was confronted with danger while being a civilian.

Back from Nam

The heading in the newspaper said, "Armed Bandits rob Sears store, and the clerk, who had returned recently from Vietnam, was the son of a police captain and the nephew of a police Sgt." A photo shows me along with a lieutenant and a tow truck driver, watching handcuffs being cut off this victim, which had been put on him by the bandits before they left the store.

* * *

The following story relates just how far some people will go to fill their pockets. This particular case was a surprise including who his accomplice was.

In a bank robbery this particular holdup man hit the same bank again. When I asked the teller for a description, she replied, "I know who he is. Is the man who held me up last time in jail?" We told her that he was. She went on to say, "It was him, I'm sure!"

We went to his last known address and found him upstairs in his bedroom, counting the money on his bed. We asked him why he would be stupid enough to rob the same bank again. His reply was, "My lawyer was pressing me for money. I'm out of jail on appeal. 'Where am I going to get the money?' I asked him. 'The same place you got it before. They will never know you,' he answered. "I hid the shotgun in his office before I went home with the loot from the bank." The attorney was arrested and the FBI found the shotgun in his office.

106

* * *

Sometimes you confront an individual while on the job as the following stories relate but death was near!

There was an armed robbery of a super market in the suburbs, in which one of the holdup men had a carbine. While following up on this, we managed to arrest one of the suspects at gunpoint while he was having a barbecue in the backyard with his relatives.

I remember taking him out of the yard in handcuffs while his family watched, and little did anyone know that this young man would be dead within a month, from a drug overdose.

* * *

In this next happening the plans of these men went haywire as their plot was frustrated.

A heading in the local papers told the story about police thwarting an elaborate getaway. "The scheme involved three getaway cars and a change of clothing, but ended up foiled, after a witness saw three bank bandit suspects switch to the second vehicle. Det. Sgt. Chernetsky, of the robbery squad, said, 'Two gunmen entered the Marine Midland bank, brushed past several customers, and announced a stickup. After the holdup, a maroon getaway car roared away, and the bandits later switched to a gold-colored auto that reportedly belonged to one of the robbers' girlfriends.'

"A witness saw the masked men making the switch and a moment later, the police radio put out an alert for a gold Camero. Police said, 'The holdup men were on the way to the suburbs, where they intended to switch to a third getaway car, and they were finally arrested, before they could complete the end of their plans.'"

* * *

Good Citizen
In the next case, a citizen goes into action!

The newspapers wrote up the story in the following manner thereby giving this citizen praise. "A spunky bank teller, tails bandits in a $4,000 bank job in which the thugs brandished a sawed-off shotgun or rifle, and the other drew a pistol when they held up the bank.

"The teller was returning to work from lunch, when she saw the gunmen fleeing from the bank, and chased the two bandits, for almost a mile, in her auto. 'She was determined to get them,' acting Lt. Michael Chernetsky, of the robbery squad declared, 'but she backed off when the car stopped and one of the gunmen got out and moved menacingly towards her auto.'"

It was sometime later that a stolen car was recovered containing the ski mask and gloves which the holdup men wore when they committed the bank robbery. They were never caught!

* * *

In this next incident we had to track down two holdup men who stuck up a furrier. The story went this way: There was a call of an afternoon holdup of a furrier store located in the downtown area of the city. Two holdup men entered the store and beat the owner and his wife. The husband was knocked to the floor while money was taken from his pockets. They took furs from the store and left the premises thereby fleeing down the street.

After our investigation, we were able to track down one of the suspects and arrested him at gunpoint. We found out the name of his accomplice and with this new information we put together a photo array, and showed the victims a series of mug shots and they identified him. This particular man received a sentence of 10 to 15 years after a jury trial.

* * *

Robberies on Whole East Coast

In this next case, a newspaper stated, "Three masked men rob Liberty Bank, wearing halloween masks, and escaped with an undetermined amount of money, after forcing customers and employees, to lie on the floor. A customer in the bank also tried to follow the bandits' car with his own vehicle, but he abandoned the chase, police said, when one of the holdup men shot at him through the rear window of the getaway car.

"Sgt. Chernetsky, one of the first officers on the scene, stated, 'Masked men walked into the bank, and ordered about 15 persons, including employees and customers, to lie on the floor. The getaway car ended up a short distance away and money was in both the front and back seats. The rear window of the car was knocked out leaving us to believe that they left the vehicle in a hurry.'"

We found out months later that they were part of a team of holdup men who were robbing stores on the East Coast, and according to FBI sources they have never been caught.

* * *

In this next story I obtained credit for a long-distance run I made.

Good Foot Chase

The newspaper headline said, "Wedding plans will have to wait for a bondsman, and that a fleeting police officer, and a doubting judge, were obstacles for a suspect who had twenty-five previous arrests, in which case the judge would not let him out on bail, even for a Christmas wedding."

His attorney said, "While this is the season for angels, I know I am not representing one but would like him released without bail," in his statement to the courts.

The article went on to say, "Detective Chernetsky, caught him after a foot chase, through heavy downtown traffic, after the suspect stole some men's suits from a downtown department store."

A reader wrote into the local newspaper about the above story and she stated, "The Buffalo Bills football team could use a good running halfback, like the detective." *How about that!*

* * *

Prisoner of War!

We arrested two robbery suspects at this particular address and during the course of making this arrest, an unknown person tossed bottles at us. One of the bottles struck me on the side of the head but I didn't require medical attention.

It wasn't because that they were friends of the suspects, it was that we were the police and we didn't belong there. It was like a sport to them, to see if they could get the suspects away from us. One of the men said to me, "Anytime I end up being busted, I say to myself, I am not being arrested, I am a prisoner of war!"

* * *

The next event brings about the lengths we will go to get a man.

It Was a Long Search but We Got Him

If you follow the course of get-a-man, mentioned previously, you get him through his girl, or his car, or his wallet, or, whichever order he finds dearest to his lifestyle.

The background on this investigation was that there was an armed robbery of a local supermarket. The description given by a witness at the holdup scene said it was a 1968 Chevy but they did not obtain a plate number.

We found the car after a long search. It happened to be a 1968 model Chevy that would normally stand out anyway due to the year. The license plate on this car didn't make any sense. Sometimes holdup men will steal a set of plates, cut them in half and then put such pairs on whatever vehicle they are using for the particular crime they do.

We staked out the car for several days! Finally a woman came to the car. We confronted her. She stated that the car belonged to her boyfriend. She told us what was said in her apartment. "They bragged about it while they divided up the money. I had nothing to do with it."

We got the girl, we got the car.

We checked out the apartment previously, under the pretext that we were looking for someone else, and at that time a woman had answered the door and we realized that our man was not present; however, she bought our story and probably didn't find it necessary to tell him. We even showed her a mug shot of another individual so her guard would not be up. We got the layout of the interior of the apartment while engaging her in a conversation.

In the above holdup, we had to kick down the door while searching for this armed robber. We had a warrant from another case, in which the suspect had slit the throat of a priest in a Catholic church. Now, when I entered the apartment this time, upon trying to serve this warrant, I jumped up on the bed, which he currently shared with a naked woman.

Picture this, if you will! I'm on top of his bed, had my gun in my hand, and my balance was unsteady, but I said to him, "You had better not have anything underneath the blanket, but your nuts," because I figured that he had a gun. He didn't have it under the pillow, but had it close by, in the bed stand.

We arrested him for a series of armed robberies, in addition to the warrant for the cutting of the priest and we got his wallet, because when arrested he had to cough up money for an attorney to defend him.

With regard to safety to the officer while arresting an armed fugitive, was get-a-man in bed, get-a-man taking a leak.

Don't Take My Car

While still on the subject of get- a man, how about listening to this story on how we captured this one person, whom we were looking for an armed robbery.

We went to his house frequently and bothered his family. We then received a phone call from one of the new assistant district attorneys. He said to us, "We were harassing his family. Go light on him, as he is giving us information." To which I replied, "Wait a minute, he is out there doing armed robberies, and you don't want us to pick him up because he is feeding you information. *Can you believe this?*"

Get His Car!

Shortly after that conversation we went to his house again, to which we received no answer, however we knew that the nice shiny Cadillac which was parked in front of his house belonged to him.

I ordered a tow truck! When it showed up, I said to the driver, "Just pretend that you are going to tow it, and hook up to it!"

The driver then went through the motions, which caused our guy to come out the front door screaming, "You can't touch my car or me, because I am under the protection of the assistant district attorney."

We arrested him, and never received a call from this young assistant district attorney again. We weren't going to tow the car, but we knew that if he were looking out the window he would go out of control about even the thought of it being towed away. (Rules on get-a-man, remember?)

* * *

In this particular event the holdup man was concerned about being identified. There was a bank robbery, in which the holdup man approached the teller and said to her, "Don't take my picture with the bank camera, and if you do I'll blow your brains out." This was written up in the newspaper and caused us concern because we had trouble getting tellers to cooperate with us while we were investigating these bank robberies.

This will be hard for you to believe, but this is straight scoop!

In some cases, not all cases, their security told them not to do so, as they didn't want them identifying anyone, and putting the bank and their own lives on the spot. They only wanted them to make statements and appear to cooperate with the local police and the FBI, but only to go so far. It was only in a few incidents that we did find a teller who would bend their rules by cooperating more than what was proposed by the bank association.

What? You Had a Gun
We even had a fine officer who was working a second job in a bank when two men came into the bank and held it up at gunpoint. This officer engaged them in a gunfight, but waited until they were outside the bank. He managed to hit one of the cars, thereby marking it with bullet holes for future identification.

Now get this, he only had a snub-nosed revolver in this gun battle, and the holdup men had carbines, but he got into trouble with the bank people! Their objections were that they didn't like the idea he had a gun on him, and they didn't like the idea that he shot at the holdup men, because according to them, the holdup was over, the bank money is insured, and they were in fear of a lawsuit, so they didn't want any other involvement. They never thought of the possibility that in the event these two men might kill someone to prevent their capture by the police or FBI.

* * *

In this story, everyone close by answered this call.

Naked Lady with a Gun!

A call went out over the police radio, "Naked lady with a gun." As a result this caused many cars to answer the call, along with my partner and me. We came upon the scene just as this lady, who was not naked, but in a negligee, shot at a man. Even though she was half naked she was as deadly as a black widow spider. We heard the shots as we jumped from our car.

Pow!

First bullet hits boxed overcoat he was holding in front of his chest.

Pow!

Second shot hits him in the ass as he turned around to run as he was trying to get out of her line of fire by jumping off the porch.

Smoking Gun!

We were about to shoot her, but she lowered the gun, and we quickly disarmed her before she could get off another shot at him. She was armed with a .22-caliber German-made revolver, with a pearl handle. He was lucky it was only a .22-cal as the first shot would have penetrated the overcoat had the gun been of a higher caliber.

It was a lover's quarrel, and he didn't want to press charges. We arrested her for possession of the gun. A caption in the local paper stated, "Boxed overcoat stops slug but second shot finds mark," thereby explaining the above story.

* * *

Sometimes during the course of answering these calls you have a probability of being injured which happened to me.

I Was Cut

We were investigating shots fired at the police and went to their assistance. We learned that the man who fired the shots ran into this particular house. We went inside and arrested him.

A crowd of about 60 people gathered outside and confronted us when we came out of the house, thereby surrounding the police car, and they attempted to take our prisoner away from us. Someone in the crowd threw a bowie knife, which narrowly missed hitting other officers.

It was at this time that an unknown person slashed me across the wrist. I went to the emergency hospital for the cut, which was not serious.

* * *

In this next occasion I was trying to arrest an individual when

She Grabbed My Gun Arm

Let me explain. We were looking for a suspect for a string of armed robberies and happened to recheck the area around his sister's house. It was at this time I went up on her porch. I could see him through the front window. "Go around to the back of the house in the event he should run that way," I whispered to my partner. The door was ajar, and I caught him by complete surprise as I confronted him and put him spread-eagle against the wall with my weapon close to his head, but not touching it.

I must explain this to you, that if your gun is touching someone's head, or any part of his body, the individual can feel it. He knows where the weapon is, and if he knows any martial arts at all, he can spin around and turn aside the weapon and strike you. Even if the weapon discharges, it will not hit him.

I held him there, in a spread-eagle position, but just then, his sister came out of nowhere and attacked me, as she grabbed hold of my gun arm, almost causing the gun to go off!

Now, you have to picture this! Here I was holding a .357 magnum near her brother's head, and she is grabbing my gun arm! I yelled to her, "Stop, my gun might go off." I had all I could do to get her off me. I hit her with my other arm, just as my partner came in the back door and assisted me.

We put them both under arrest. I told her what she almost caused to happen, as I would have shot her brother in the head. Her response was, "I didn't think of that, I just didn't like the idea of a gun being pointed at my brother." In addition to our charges, the Niagara Falls PD (a suburb just outside Buffalo) placed two more additional charges against him after a police lineup.

* * *

Sometimes crime is up and sometimes it is down depending on the weather, economic conditions, etc. One particular month it was up as is indicated in the following story.

Crime Wave

We had a crime wave this one month, in which we had over 16 robberies at the start of the holiday season. We explained to the newspaper, "We have a lot of them every year at this time, as these guys need money for the holidays, and they know that the tills are full this time of the year, from Thanksgiving to after New Year's."

* * *

In this next account we learn that things are not always what they appear to be.

We Don't Do This, Do We?

On this particular case, I was breaking in a new detective on the robbery squad. We were in process of arranging our cases, which was from the previous night, before we went out on the street. I am only mentioning race, at this time because we had a report of an individual who stated that he was mugged in a certain section of the city by a group of black males. My partner at that particular time happened to be black, and it had a bearing on the case.

We talked with the man in his house, in front of his wife, and he related the story again. I got the feeling that something wasn't right, because he was very nervous talking in front of my partner. Too nervous!

I asked him to come outside, so that his wife wouldn't hear us. I said to him, "I don't believe you. Your story about being robbed at that time and that section of the city doesn't hold water. Tell me the real story! What did you do with the money?"

My partner looked at me and said "We don't do this, do we?"

Our victim's final answer was, "I made up the robbery to cover money I lost in gambling, so that I wouldn't have to tell my wife the truth." We arrested him for filing a false crime report.

* * *

Like the Wild West

In this next event there had been a series of armed robberies in the city which were reminiscent of the Wild West. The gunmen would board a bus and hold up the passengers as well as the drivers. Things were so bad that one bus driver happened to be a victim three times over a period of seven months, thereby causing the bus companies to be very nervous.

In this one robbery, a woman passenger refused to give up her purse and scuffled with one of the holdup men, causing his partner in crime to come to his assistance. This man ended up accidentally shooting and killing his partner. Two other woman passengers feared reprisals and refused to tell the police anything, stating that they just wanted to go home.

In another related robbery, a bus driver ended up shot in the face and the abdomen, after three boys boarded his bus and robbed him at gunpoint.

In another holdup, a driver was shot after he attacked his first assailant, knocking him off the bus.

After an intense investigation, we managed to hunt down one of the suspects and took him into custody. An hour later, the other man turned himself in to a local news agency after his mother told the media, "I was afraid that the police would kill my son, so I turned him in."

* * *

Sometimes you have to go to various places to pick up prisoners. On this occasion we went to Minneapolis, Minnesota.

The newspapers wrote the story this way: "The police picked up a man, who escaped while at a city court appearance last June, and was returned to city court and arraigned on an escape count, after the suspect was recaptured in Minneapolis, Minn. and brought back to Buffalo by Sgt. Schwartz and Sgt. Chernetsky of the Buffalo police."

It was weird because several years later, we met this defendant again. He charged the front door of a restaurant, wearing just black pajamas and carrying a large sword, like a ninja warrior. We answered the radio call and showed up just in time. We prevented him from entering the restaurant and probably saved his life. The restaurant owner was armed, and told us later, "I would have blown him away if he would have come in the door, but lucky you stopped him."

About one year after this, we were in this same restaurant, and again, this same individual enters, but this time, instead of a sword, he is carrying a Bible and is trying to preach to us to mend our ways. (Can you believe this?)

* * *

Armed and Dangerous Women

We were looking for a woman who was committing armed robberies of various small stores. We went to her residence to try to apprehend her, and knocked on the door. A woman answered. We asked her if the person we were looking for was living there. Although she replied in the negative, her gestures told us something different. She said "No" but nodded "Yes" and pointed to a rear bedroom, which was in view. This led us to believe that the woman we wanted was in fact, in that particular bedroom. I went in there and didn't see anyone, and then decided to pull up one end of the bed and look underneath, while at the same time sticking my gun underneath. It's a good thing that I did this, as the woman was lying belly down, with a gun in her hand, pointed my way. When she saw the barrel of my gun, she released the grip on hers and came out from under the bed with her hands up.

I was lucky again, don't you think?

* * *

Bubble Gum Bandit

In still another instance, we arrested an East Side housewife identified as the "Bubble gum bandit." She would hold up small delicatessens at gunpoint, and in so doing, entered the stores, looked around, and then ordered bubble gum, along with some other small articles. She pulled out a gun, and said,

"This is holdup." Her hair was dyed to a sandy color, to avoid recognition by anyone while she was doing these holdups.

We canvassed the area for several hours, before we finally located her and put her under arrest. The local newspapers printed her picture in the paper, with the caption: "Bubble Gum Bandit Captured."

* * *

In this next occurrence some young punks decided that an old man would be an easy target.

He Was 84 and They Beat Him

There was an 84-year-old man who would never hurt anybody. He was beaten and robbed in the middle of the night by four youths. One of them practiced his karate by repeatedly kicking him. A close relative found him in the morning when he came there to check up on him.

It was our case and we proceeded to interview the victim. During the course of this investigation we looked around the living room. "Look, there is a button on the floor, is it yours?" I asked.

The victim answered, "It's not mine. It must have come off one of the holdup men during the struggle." *Little did we know at the time, that the finding of this button would help us solve this case!*

We solved this case by leads from the neighborhood and the button. It happened to match one of the buttons missing from a youth's jacket, whom we questioned in a local pool hall. We arrested four suspects! One of them was a 15-year-old juvenile, and the others were adults.

One of the adults did ten years on a molestation charge on a juvenile in another matter. Would you believe that this adult even had our victim's watch on when we arrested him? He was the brave karate expert who kicked the old man!

* * *

We Can Take This Cop Down

There was a situation when we noticed that one of our beat officers was having an argument with three individuals on the corner, who appeared to be giving him a hard time. We knew this officer, and that he was quite capable of taking care of himself, but we decided to hang around and be ready in the event he needed backup.

We were in plain clothes and situated ourselves so that we would be able to help him out if the need should arise. We overheard him tell the three men, who appeared to be loitering, "Get off the corner! If I find you guys hanging around there when I get back from walking my beat, I'll arrest you!" He turned his back on them and walked away to continue his beat patrol. He was unaware of the danger that was to come upon him.

Joe and I just happened to overhear a remark, when one of the three men said to the others, "Let's get up behind him, hit him, and take his gun away." They all agreed on doing this, and started to follow the officer. But just when they were upon him, he sensed them and started to turn to protect himself. It was at this time that Joe and I jumped the men and told the officer what they had intended to do. They all resisted arrest, and we had quite a fight on the street before we were able to handcuff them.

However, later during the course of a trial, two of the three pled guilty. But it wasn't until a year later, to the day, that one other individual ended up taking a reduced plea, which saved the courts the expense of taking this case to trial.

* * *

The following cases are related to dogs, some of which were on the premises of the persons we were trying to arrest.

Going to the Dogs

The story in the local newspaper stated, "One doggoned robbery case, left the police, barking up the wrong tree."

The background of the story is as follows: A man fit the exact description of the holdup suspect, and was running with a dog after he fled the robbery scene. The dog in question was described as a Doberman pinscher, who as indicated, was thought to be running with the holdup man, away from the scene of this armed robbery.

We searched the immediate area looking for the holdup man. We thought we had the right man and right dog, but as it ended up, we had the right dog but the wrong man. Our man indicated that he was going by the scene of the robbery at the same time that the holdup man was coming out, which led our witness to be confused about the description, except for the dog, which they thought belonged to the man who held up the place.

* * *

Twin Dogs

In another case, we were looking to catch this individual for an armed robbery for which we had a warrant. But every time we went to his house, he was not at home. There was always a large, white German shepherd dog in the window when we went up on the porch, but it was in the downstairs part of the house. We figured that if we could see the dog in the window we were safe, as our man lived upstairs and he always has his dog with him.

On this particular day, we tried the house again and noted that the dog was downstairs in the window as usual, but this time we received an answer at the door and it was our suspect. We told him that he was under arrest, but just then another dog came charging at us, a white German shepherd, the same description as the one downstairs.

We drew our guns. "Hold the dog back," we both said, "or we'll shoot him."

This action caused our man to control the dog by holding the animal by the tail, and screaming at us, "Please don't shoot my dog."

We put him under arrest! We later found out that there actually were two white German shepherds, as this dog was a twin to the dog which had appeared at the downstairs window.

* * *

Attack Dogs

I want to mention that in this incident, we had an additional case of dealing with a dog while we were looking for a certain suspect who had dogs in his house.

A caption in the local paper wrote up the story this way: "Chernetsky called for backup, when he learned there was a Doberman dog, trained to attack, in the suspect's house. The Sgt. said that he had to shove a washer and a dryer, in front of a door in the house, to keep an attack dog at bay."

The explanation to the story was, we arrested him at his home, but had to call for a backup, as signs posted around his house indicated that he had an attack dog. It was when we entered the house that we heard the dog barking and asked him to restrain his animal. He smiled and put the dog (another Doberman) in a bathroom. However, the door swung out, and the dog was beginning to get out at us.

As indicated in the newspaper, we had to push a washer and a dryer against the bathroom door, which kept the dog at bay!

* * *

In the next story the police are confronted with a lot of firepower in an investigation.

According to a newspaper article, there were 30 shots fired at the police, while two detectives answered a call of "Shots fired and gang activity." One person ended up cut during a fight over drugs and during the course of their investigation, the detectives obtained some names from these youths.

Later they saw one of the persons named by the victim getting into a car which was parked at the curb. There were four men inside it, and one of them was at the trunk of the car. After the plainclothes officers identified themselves, the suspect at the trunk pulled out an assault rifle and began firing at them. Another suspect pulled out a handgun, and then there was an exchange of gunfire at this particular corner, in which some 30 shots exchanged.

It's a good thing that the detectives were armed with 9mm automatics because they were able to return the firepower. Two of the men escaped and sped away.

My partner and I spotted the car used in the shooting, because of bullet holes in the rear window, which made it easy to identify. When we heard a call go out over the air about a man shot, we figured that this is probably one of our guys. My partner and I went into the house and found him lying on the floor in an upstairs bedroom. He told us, "I was spread eagle at the trunk of the car when the gunfire started and had nothing to do with the shooting. It was my friends who fired at the detectives."

We called the detectives who were involved in this shooting, and when they came over, they took one look at him and said, "Yep, that's the guy who shot at us."

* * *

New York Times Call

On May 17, 1975, the *New York Times* called to inquire about juvenile holdup men who were robbing banks here in Buffalo. There was an article in the *Times* dated 5-17-75 by Robert D. McFadden in which I was quoted.

Two 15-year-old youths held up a local bank at gunpoint and escaped with $10,000.

The story made the local papers, in an article which stated, "Detective Sgt. Michael Chernetsky, of the Buffalo robbery squad, described justice for juvenile offenders as a revolving door, stating that these kids know we can't touch them, and they defy us." One 15-year-old boy held another bank up for $10,500. Four other youths ended up under arrest in the bank heists.

My partner and I, along with agents of the FBI, searched a downtown hotel and sealed it off. On the ninth floor, we got one of them, who then implicated the others in the bank robbery.

This account ended up written up in our local newspaper as follows, "Police arrested four youths and recovered $4500, in a Delaware Avenue hotel." Three of the suspects ended up arrested in a room at 210 Delaware Avenue, after we sealed off the building and searched door to door.

The paper indicated that "Sgt. Chernetsky and others from the robbery squad, along with agents of the FBI, got off a ninth-floor elevator when the door opened to reveal a juvenile suspected of other bank robberies. The money reportedly was found stashed in a false ceiling and also other money was hidden in the socks of one of the juveniles who were arrested."

In yet an additional incident, we arrested an 15-year-old boy, while he was riding in a taxicab and we charged him with taking part in a bank robbery.

Other officers recovered a sawed-off .22-caliber rifle believed to be the weapon used in the holdup. It was noted that this particular bank robbery was the 27th bank robbery of this year, compared with ten at this time the previous year.

Further investigation disclosed that one 16-year-old youth pled guilty to killing two men in two different holdups. They were passing out money to relatives, and word on the street got back to us that one of the murderers did a previous drug store holdup.

* * *

How many times would you be confronted with an individual you kept putting in jail? Read the following story about an unusual situation relative to this matter.

Three Strikes and You're Out

A writeup in the paper read, "Detective arrests man for the third time in ten years, (*Courier Express*, September 13, 1975)[20] and when he saw me he cried big tears," Detective Chernetsky said. My picture was in the newspaper concerning this event, along with the following story, in which the article in the paper continued with, "Old Nemesis Nabs Robbery Suspect. (John Doe, I am using this name to protect the identity of the real individual.)

"John Doe, of Peter St. wasn't a bit happy when he ran into an old acquaintance the other night. Det. Sgt. Michael Chernetsky of the Robbery Squad arrested him. It was the third time that Chernetsky arrested him in 10 years. John Doe, age 35, was arrested Thursday night, near a clam stand by Chernetsky and his partner, also of the robbery squad," the story in the newspaper stated.

The events leading up to this story were as follows:

I was working with a different partner that particular tour of duty, and we entered this bar looking for an unnamed suspect. We were here because the information given to us stated that this unnamed individual was going to hold up this particular place.

Upon our entry in the bar we separated. I had taken off my coat and put my gun underneath it on top of the bar, because if it was the same man we thought it was, he would hold up the bar and then line all the patrons up and take their property also.

A barmaid came in and spoke to me, indicating that she knew who I was, but wanted to warn me that the guy I was looking for was now outside holding up the clam stand, because she saw a gun and was about to call 911.

I told my partner to go out the front, and I would come around the side, and this way we would catch him in the middle. But when I came out the side door, I saw that my partner had moved in too soon, because he already had his gun to the suspect's head. However, what he didn't know was that the suspect could easily move my partner's gun hand from his head and fire underneath his own armpit, as he had his gun in his waistband.

I had my 9mm gun pointed straight towards him and it was then that I recognized him and called to him by name. "Charlie, don't move!" I yelled! I knew that I could shoot him without hitting my partner.

He looked over at me, and at my 9mm pointed at him, thereby dropping his weapon that he was reaching for and cried out to me, "Oh, no, not you again."

I arrested him in 1965 for auto theft, and in 1971 in connection with a series of liquor store robberies. The auto theft charges resulted in a six-month term in the county pen, while the 1971 arrest resulted in a sentence up to five years at a narcotic treatment center. It was hard to believe that he would pull these holdups in only an hour after he had just made a necessary visit to his parole officer.

(See previous story, where I received Officer of the Month for this, along with my partner, Joe.)

The paper went on to say, "That the latest confrontation with Chernetsky resulted with a warrant charging that he robbed a local store. A lineup was held and he was charged with other robberies, and the Tonawanda Police (a suburb near Buffalo) lodged a reckless endangerment warrant against him for firing four shots into a tavern where he got into an argument over a pool game."

The same newspaper article said, "After capturing him, the detective said he took from him a revolver that had been reported as stolen by a retired Lockport policeman."

Would You Believe Four Times?

I ran into him again, for a fourth time, when I was in a situation when we had to call our SWAT team, as this was mentioned in a previous chapter where I had gone to the corner store for the newspaper.

* * *

On this next occasion I was taking a prisoner back to be booked when it took an unexpected turn of events

I Was Knocked out of the Car

On this particular circumstance, I was in the back seat of the patrol car, and had a prisoner seated next to me, but not behind the driver, which was the procedure. It was daytime, traffic was heavy, and a tactical unit followed behind us as backup, because this person had pulled several armed robberies in which he fired shots. All of a sudden, he kicked his feet off from the right side of the car, and hits me with his back, and with the force of his legs, forces me right out the door taking me with him.

When we hit the pavement, I was on the bottom, and he was on the top, but even though he was cuffed with his hands behind his back, he managed to fight like hell, thereby kicking and throwing his body around as we both lay there in the street with traffic going by us. The backup car was on him, and he continued fighting while being hit by billy clubs and I ended up being struck several times during the course of this struggle (unavoidable).

* * *

On this particular search for an armed felon I was lucky to spot his car but it was in the suburbs and I was alone. It was at his mother's house. I have to say that if I knew for sure that he would be there I would have had more men with me at that time.

I called for a backup from the Amherst Police Department (a suburb of Buffalo), and informed the uniformed officer of the circumstances surrounding this case, since this individual had shot at other people before, and showed him his mug shot. Because we were afraid that he would look out and see the cars, we went in without waiting for additional backup.

This officer went to the front door, and I went to the side and went into the house, just as some young person was leaving. I asked her if her uncle was there, and she said, "Yes, he is lying on the couch." I had to act quickly before being discovered, so I took full advantage of the situation and ran into the dining room.

There he was belly down on the couch, as she stated. I had my weapon raised towards him, ready to shoot if necessary, because I thought the suspect had a gun underneath him, but he had none and came quietly. I opened the front door and let the officer in, and explained that I managed to gain excess through the open door, and was lucky enough to take him into custody with out any trouble. I was visibly nervous as I thought I would have to shoot him in front of the little girl.

* * *

This story is about an unusual chase which started in Buffalo and left our jurisdiction.

Chased Bank Robbers from Buffalo to Rochester

A local newspaper here in Buffalo showed a picture of Joe and me, and the head of the FBI (Neil Welch) here in Buffalo. This picture was in the *Courier Express* dated March 29, 1970, which showed us with money fanned out in our hands as results of chasing bank robbers from Buffalo to Rochester. We had a tip from an informant!

Before we left, we had a staff meeting, along with the FBI and the chief of detectives here in Buffalo (Ralph V. Degenhart[21]), so as to be briefed on what to expect in this raid. My partner, Joe, gave them a rundown on who were looking for, and indicated to the group present at this meeting, "One of the men had killed before, and would possibly kill again." He then went on to say, "Two bank employees and a customer were pistol-whipped in this particular bank robbery. They recovered after treatment in a local hospital."

We arrived in Rochester and the cabbie then pointed out the house he left them off at, even though they had a four-hour head start. Joe and I were surprised to see some of the agents opening up suitcases that contained shotguns, which made us feel naked as we had only handguns. We took down the door and entered the house and caught them by complete surprise, as we seized the suspects in the kitchen with the bank money on the kitchen table.

* * *

Said He Wouldn't Be Taken Alive

There are some occasions when an individual brags that they will not be taken alive. Of course this will make the average officer more wary when you are about to confront this individual.

There was a man sought for ten months on a robbery and shooting in a tavern. A caption in the paper indicated, "The arrest was fast and cautious by the robbery squad, who said the man told others there is 'No way he would come in alive.'

"Sgt. Chernetsky said, 'The unlawful imprisonment charges stem from a motorist who was forced at gunpoint to drive the four bandits to the robbery scene, where they locked him in the trunk of the auto and abandoned it. This motorist died in August of that year at a military recruit camp in Texas.'"

"You never know when death is around the corner."

* * *

You Have to Buy It

If the city won't buy it, you buy it, if you want to survive!

There came a time that I decided to buy a 9mm semiautomatic pistol S&W model, because the department was not using them. I bought it as a backup gun because the street was rough at that time. You came to realize that the holdup men were better armed than we were.

Years, later I purchased a 9mm Glock, with my own money. I also bought a bulletproof vest, even though the department was not using them at that time.

The criminals on the street were outgunning us and it was only common sense to try to protect yourself anyway you can. I was ahead of the times, because some years later the department issued bulletproof vests and 9mm semiautomatics to officers.

* * *

We Witnessed a Mugging

We came upon two men mugging a man in the downtown sector of the city. As soon as they saw us, they split up, with me chasing one of them and my partner chasing the other. During the chase I fired one warning shot (I could have legally shot him!) and chased him behind a dark building and into a vacant lot. While back there, I fell into a hole and ended up pulling a muscle in my thigh.

However, I continued in the chase and pursued him into a backyard, where he attempted to climb an eight-foot fence. I was unable to climb the fence, and had my gun pointed at him while yelling to him, "I'll shoot if you don't come down." His answer was "Go ahead." He started to drop to the other side, but another officer, who was on that side of the fence, apprehended him. While being booked it was discovered that he had marijuana on his person.

Like Chester on *Gunsmoke*!

Here is an addition to this story by a citizen who witnessed this event go down. I spoke with her on one of my other jobs. She told me, "I wondered what was up when I saw you limping down the street, like Chester on *Gunsmoke*, and then I saw you chasing the man, and you had your gun drawn, and I heard the shot go off." I explained the story to her.

* * *

This crime bugged me for a long time. The following story is about a case in which I could not give up on the answer to the following questions:

What happened to the reverend?

Was he killed?

Was he missing?

There was a picture on the front page of a newspaper, which shows me seated at my desk, while at my typewriter, and articles which I had looked over numerous times. They consisted of a Bible, (Lord's Prayer written inside the cover), snapshots of children, and a young adult, which I had obtained in an arrest I made a year earlier (August 14, 1981).

128

I found the following words written inside the Bible, "REV. W[22] 815 N6th St. Kennedy Bldg. Apt. 913," but there was no city or state listed. This led me to wonder if he was dead, or the victim of a crime. I just didn't have the answer and it bugged me for over a year, which the article in the paper indicated. I wouldn't give up on the case!

It started when I arrested a man who was in possession of this property, while working a second job at a downtown hotel. I found him in the men's room with a large suitcase. Upon checking further, we found he was not registered at this hotel and the articles in the suitcase did not appear to belong to him.

He went to court and admitted that he stole items from a suitcase which was in a bus station in his hometown of Pittsburgh, Pennsylvania. But a check with the police there disclosed that the suspect was known there but there was no record of a larceny in the bus terminal or of a Rev. W. living there.

The man I arrested left Buffalo after pleading guilty, but without the items in the suitcase, including the pictures, etc., which remained in police possession.

There were no more leads, and I set these items aside. I often wondered what happened to the reverend because it really bothered me. I thought that perhaps he may have been a victim of a crime, or even killed by this individual.

In continuing about the article in the newspaper, it stated further: "The Sgt. kept an eye on various police communications, and a break came in August of 1982." It wasn't easy to pick up on this case; after all, the value of a Bible and some photographs are small, unless they are yours. "His regular work with robbery took a lot of his days and then classes at Buffalo State College, where he is working towards a degree in education, took a lot of his free time."

I found a piece of paper about a bank account and it was from Steubenville, Ohio. Since there was no name I had made the assumption that it could have belonged to our suspect. I wrote them a letter, on official stationary, giving the Rev. W's full name and the response was long coming in that they had him as a depositor but would say no more as it was confidential. But now I knew that he was from that city and state. I got in touch with the Steubenville, Ohio, phone listings again, for a list of all the Rev. W's living there.

The newspaper article went on to say, "Would you believe the first number I called, turned out to be his daughter-in-law,' Sgt. Chernetsky said. From her he learned why his calls to the man were not answered, the Rev. W., age 80, was seriously ill, and had been in a nursing home for months. Mrs.... said a man had duped his way into her father-in-law's apartment and stole the items, plus clothing and money last year." The article continued with, "It was exactly one year to the day, after he made the arrest, and confiscated the items that Sgt. Chernetsky mailed them to the minister's daughter-in-law. The snapshots were of the grandchildren, he was told, and with the package in the mail, the 45-year-old sergeant, who counts 20 years on the force (13 with the robbery squad), closed another case."

* * *

Who Fired the Gun?

In this next occurrence we answered a call of a holdup in a liquor store. The victim had six bullet holes in him, and was still alive. An ambulance came to the scene. Newspaper accounts of this story indicated that the holdup men fired nine shots, six of which struck the victim.

We questioned the victim's wife, and she told us that two men came into the store, armed with guns, and tried to hold them up. This is when her husband was shot. There was blood on the floor outside the enclosed wire mesh cage designed to protect the owners of the store. The victim's wife was asked about it. "My husband must have fired his gun, and hit one of the holdup men in the exchange of gunfire in the store," she explained. We noticed a gun lying on the floor, asked her if she touched it, to which she replied that she had not.

We found out that after the shooting of her husband, she did in fact pick up the gun and started shooting at the holdup men. Both holdup men had gone to the hospital. One suspect sought treatment for five bullet holes, one of them in the genitals. He ended up at the same hospital as the victim.

How she managed to hit both of them while shooting from the other side of a mesh cage is still a mystery. You will have to admit, that was some shooting by a woman who said that she never fired a gun before.

* * *

In this next incident I was involved in a conflict with a local TV news station.

Who's the Bad Guy Here?

We spotted a taxi going into a local television station parking lot. When we pulled it over we could see that the man in the back seat ducked down. It was a violent man whom we had been searching for. We arrested him at gunpoint.

TV people were filming the capture, because unknown to us, they had set up a meet with this criminal. They yelled to us this was unfair because we messed up their scoop. They were starting to get in our way, so I told them, "If you want to get good pictures, how about taking pictures of me busting your boss for obstruction."

They had given this criminal a prior interview, in which they had allowed him to proclaim his innocence. He was a wanted man then, and they claimed they didn't know that. This drew harsh criticism from the police commissioner. The media claimed that they called someone at the DA's office and were informed that he was not wanted. We could never find out who they allegedly spoke to at that time.

People in the neighborhood, where the woman died and the man was beaten, protested to this event being on TV the first time. They said that it was a slap in the face for decent people who lived in the area of the crime.

It was because the media were trying to boost their ratings at the expense of the victims of crimes. This man was bitter because of his wife's death after the robbery. His wife was 67 at the time of the beating, and he was 91. The robbery was September of 1981 and this was April of 1982, but the DA couldn't prove her death was as a result the robbery and beatings.

In addition, speaking of a slap in the face, the news people were so mad at us out-scooping them, that they showed a picture of me on TV with my gun in the criminal's face. I got sick of seeing it, as they would show it every now and then. I talked of suing them, but I was told since I was a public figure and it was on the evening news, I could not do so!

Officer's Gun?

They even had their investigative reporter go over to the commissioner and ask why I was carrying a semiautomatic. Never mind that this guy beat an old lady to death, or beat up her husband: "We want to know why the officer was carrying an unauthorized weapon?"

Well, it didn't work. The commissioner at that time stuck up for me, and stated that the officer was carrying his on-duty gun and a backup gun (Thank God for the back up gun!) which is legal, and he happened to have reached for that one first. End of story!

I managed to take a picture off the TV of this particular incident, i.e. them showing me making this particular arrest with my gun pointed at the suspect's head, and I still have it for a keepsake.

Vigilantes

We answered a call of a fight in the street. Our arrival was just in time, because we were about to witness a beating of two men by a mob. I jumped out of my vehicle and blocked the arm of a vigilante who tried to bash this man's head in, thereby disarming him. (I almost got my head bashed in for this!)

Naturally, the robbers were happy to surrender to us, and of course I didn't have a score card at that time, and didn't know who was who, but I would not have allowed someone to be assaulted in my presence anyway, no matter what.

We put the two house painters in for an award and they obtained official recognition for personal responsibility to justice, when they caught a pair of muggers. They even offered the man protection when he went to court, in the event there was retribution to his testimony.

The picture in the local paper showed the two men with me and the head of the robbery squad, along with my partner at that time of the arrest, as we presented them with the award.

* * *

You would think that an officer responding to a call would not be taken prisoner, especially since other police cars had responded to this call. Listen to the following story relative to this strange series of events.

A car crew containing two patrol officers responded to a call of an armed robbery of a local supermarket. The holdup men used a machine gun and a carbine. The officers spotted the getaway car, a blue station wagon, as this was the description which was given out by the police dispatcher. The car was empty when it was found abandoned with stolen plates attached to it. Then the police radio dispatcher put out a description of a red van with ladders on it. When this went out over the air, a patrolman recalled this description of the van and put out the name of the man he last saw in it. He had seen this van several weeks before this holdup.

A certain tactical officer was riding alone and spotted it with the ladders and called for a backup. Something went wrong! The suspect took this officer hostage, along with his police car. Responding police units who were coming up to the intersection after the first gunfire assumed that everything was okay, because of seeing the police car parked in front, had then pulled away. They didn't know that the officer was taken hostage, along with the police car he was riding in.

Some half-hour later, the holdup man let the officer go, after taking the officer's gun, and was now running on foot through various backyards.

We arrived on the scene and were helping in the search of the backyards, aware of the fact that the suspect had a .357 magnum, which he took from the officer. (This criminal's machine gun jammed; that is why he took the officers gun.)

Now, you will have to visualize the series of uncanny events that transpired after this police chase appeared to be coming to a climax.

At this time, one of our other detective cars pulled up to the scene, with two detectives in the front seat, and one detective in the back seat.

Couldn't Get out of the Seat

When being confronted with this armed suspect, the detectives in the front seat managed to bail out of the car while being shot at by the holdup man. However, the detective in the back seat was not able to bail out, as the locks were secure due to having prisoners in the rear seat at times. He couldn't get out of the car, as the gunman opened fire on the car and bullets were crashing through the windshield.

This detective returned fire back through the windshield, while still sitting in the back seat dodging bullets! The suspect was wounded by other detectives, but fled the immediate area, and was later captured after he threw his gun down.

The detective in the back seat received a reward for his courage.

* * *

The following incident describes when people are lured into various street scams. I arrested a man who was enticing a woman into playing a no-win card game, even though the woman told him that she was not interested. He grabbed her money anyway. There was a writeup in the paper where I was quoted, "It's like the old pea shell routine," explaining youths often try to trick people into playing the game along downtown streets, invariably resulting in the player losing his money.

I was surprised when I arrested him on a warrant several years later because the house in which I arrested him was the one in which I was born. This was another weird coincidence. *Remember at the beginning of this book, I arrested and chased a man into a house where I grew up.*

On Camera

A photograph taken by a bank camera led to the arrest of three suspects in the holdup of a bank. During the arrest, three syringes, hypodermic needles, and a cooker with residue of alleged heroin were seized. According to the caption in a local paper, "Sgt. Chernetsky and Schwartz recognized the holdup men from the picture taken by the bank camera, and arrested all three at their home."

There were many letters of commendations, some from the police department, and others from the FBI, for the work we did on bank robberies.

So, there you have it. The whole series of crimes against the person, in which the robbery squad was responsible. We covered the whole city and answered these calls along with hot calls to assist the patrol force.

What happens when you are working a second job and a crime occurs in your presence? Find out in the next chapter.

Chapter Twenty-Two
Second Jobs

Police officers work one or two jobs in addition to their police job because of the low salary they get. I have worked quite a few second fronts (second jobs) over a period of years while I was a police officer and have listed some of them below.

* * *

There was security in various stores in the downtown area malls, which consisted of a woman's clothing store, a record store, and a department store.

I also worked in a security capacity for a local food chain, which consisted of guarding the money in the main office and keeping the general peace in the store while being on the lookout for theft.

Then there was a job for a trucking company, which consisted of both being a driver and loading trucks. At another trucking agency I drove their drivers to a downtown hotel so they wouldn't get lost or end up in the wrong neighborhood while seeking lodging.

Another assignment was guarding persons who were on their way to work at a factory. This was in the early hours of the morning, because a few of them were victims of muggings in the parking lot.

I worked security for a new hotel being built in downtown Buffalo and continued in their employ after it was completed and opened for the public.

There was even a job as a pallbearer for the father of one of the detectives I worked with who ran a funeral home and needed people on short notice.

I Worked as a Private Eye

These events happened to me while I was working as a private investigator for a detective agency by the name of William Burns International Detective Agency. I served in that capacity from 1962 to 1968. It was a fun job and it was a change from the police routine.

While working for this agency I went to various hospitals to see how they functioned with regard to the security of the narcotics cabinets where all the drugs are kept. While doing this, at one particular hospital, I learned that there was a rape of a young nurse and the administration officials said that we would have to keep this quiet, and not to call the police, because they didn't want the adverse publicity. "I'm sorry," I said, "you can't do that." In addition to the job for the detective agency, I was also a police officer for the city of Buffalo, and didn't think their decision was wise. I found out that it was a maintenance man who worked in the hospital and that he had a rap sheet. I obtained his mug shot and put it in with a series of others, and she identified his picture. I made the arrest without a warrant because it had just occurred. It's a good thing that I acted this way, because her father was a very high-ranking officer in SAC (Strategic Air Command). He was on his way to Buffalo to see about his daughter. I mean it didn't make any difference to me, case solved, but can you imagine if the crime was buried and he came to the hospital to see what happened to his daughter.

Union Problems

There had been some union trouble, and it started to escalate into threats of violence. The agency was informed that some of the leaders of the union and their families were being threatened by thugs. I was assigned to be part of a protection force to meet the intimidation of certain union officials. This agency assigned me to guard a union official's family while he was at work. I had to stay nights for several weeks until things cooled down.

However, on one particular occasion, a man came up the driveway at the end of my tour. I confronted him at the door and told the family to stay inside, with a warning to call for help if necessary. I didn't even show my badge, but asked him for his identification. After he sized me up and down, he readily identified himself to me, leaving me to think that he got the message. "I'm just here to make an inquiry on whether or not you needed any driveway work done. I'm doing a friend a favor by trying to get him concrete work, and thought maybe you would be a future customer," he remarked to me.

We could never prove otherwise. He then left in a hurry. I ran a check of his license plate and his name. It was determined that he had no record, and was not wanted by the police. After a while things returned to normal, as all the threats appeared to have died down, which led to the recall of all the bodyguards who were assigned for this protection force.

* * *

In this next story I was working security in another capacity in a food store chain.

Caught Him Right Away!

I was at a local super market, and at this particular time, I happened to be in uniform. (Sometimes we worked in uniform and other times in plainclothes.) A woman came up to me and stated that she had gone to her car in our parking lot, and a young man mugged her. She said, "He just went walking away down the street!" I asked her how long ago this happened, she replied, "Just now." I didn't put a call in, as I had no portable radio, and didn't want to waste time going to a payphone inside the store.

I asked her to come with me, and put her in my private vehicle and searched for this individual because I wanted her to identify him. She sat in the front seat and after a few minutes, she screamed, "There he is, that's him!"

I jumped out of my car, and even though I was in uniform I identified myself as a Buffalo police officer. I immediately put him under arrest, and searched him for a weapon. I found her credit cards!

The woman was thankful for this quick service, but I want to say at this time that it was pure luck that this individual was still in the immediate area of the crime.

* * *

Good Block!

A caption in a local newspaper stated, "Ex-boxer accused of hitting officer. He ended up arrested with a charge of knocking a police officer over a counter and creating a disturbance, inciting a riot and resisting arrest. He encouraged others in the store to battle the detective, who said, several persons in the crowd then struck him."

The police officer in the case was me and this man was a professional boxer. I was lucky because he happened to land a punch on me, that I just about blocked, the force of which knocked me over a counter.

I have to mention at this time, that I felt my experiences with judo and karate helped me ward off that punch and avoid serious injury. *(Refer to Chapter 10, Know Something.)*

* * *

Can't block them all, as I found out in this next event.

Lost a Tooth!

I was working a second job in a local mall. I spotted a man stealing records, putting them under his coat, and was about to leave the store. He was with two other men. I stopped him at the door and put him under arrest. He put up a fight, and just at this time, one of them flashed a security guard badge and tried to impress me stating, "You're not going to arrest our friend."

Now here I was facing the three of them, and I thought to myself that I can't pull my weapon, even if to scare them, and hold them at bay until help comes, because the store is too crowded, and I was in fear of hitting someone if I had to discharge my weapon.

A struggle ensued, and it was at this time, while trying to hang on to all three of them, when the first man hit me in the face with his fist and knocked out one of my front teeth, due to a huge ring on his hand. I still managed to graze him with my blackjack. It was at this time that the store people put out an "officer in trouble" call, while I still hung on to the three of them, while awaiting backup. When they arrived I informed them that the three men were under arrest, not only for the assault on me, but for the theft of the records, which started the whole thing in motion.

The result of this was that the security guard lost his job with his agency over this particular matter. A caption in the local paper said, "Officer at mall loses tooth making arrest, and in addition the officer had facial cuts and a broken wristwatch in the scuffle." This was all in a second job!

* * *

In this next situation I lost my champion image in the eyes of a little girl who used to always talk to me when she came in the store.

In the Eyes of a Child!

A little girl came into the store as usual, along with her big sister. But this time she ignored me, leaving me to wonder why! I just happened to overhear her make a remark, in which she said, "I always thought he was a nice man, until I saw him hitting someone last week."

My mind flashed back, and I recalled the incident she was referring to, but didn't know that she was aware what had occurred at that time in the store when I had this fight. This was at the same time that the city of Buffalo was in a reign of terror, as someone called the ".22-Cal Killer" was killing black men on the streets of Buffalo.

I heard a commotion up in front of the store! As I approached, I saw two black women throwing cans at this white man, who was screaming at them. I have to mention race, as it is relevant to what transpired, because I figured that they were the ones causing the trouble since they were throwing cans at someone. I was mistaken!

I was in uniform at this time, while working security in this store, and as I neared the scene, the two women pointed in another direction. I was able to hear this white man calling them vile names and making threatening gestures towards them. I noticed that he was dressed in combat gear, and looked like a soldier of some kind, and appeared to be under the influence of drugs.

I asked the women if they wanted to prefer charges against him, as I would have arrested him, but they answered with, "No, we just want to be left alone."

"Calm down," I told him. I noticed that he was with a woman who appeared to be trying to control his actions. I politely asked her, "Would you please take him out of the store?" But instead of complying with her wishes, he began to attack me. I saw he was reaching for a knife or other weapon of some kind, and I caught his arm, or the crook of it, as he tried to get into his back pocket. It ended up that he did have a knife and was going for it, and I managed to apply a hammerlock and threw him on top of the grocery conveyer belt with a judo throw. This caused his face to be jammed into the belt, thereby causing his glasses to fly off and they broke, causing bloody cuts to his face.

This is what the little girl saw! I was jumping into the frying pan again! I could have legally shot him!

It was at that time, that the police came into the store, and I informed them that he was under arrest, and also mentioned to them to check him out as a suspect in the killing of blacks here in the city of Buffalo, but further investigation disclosed that he was not the man.

I made my peace with the little girl, but only after her aunt explained to her what had happened.

* * *

This circumstance explains a situation that developed in a store I was guarding when a man made the mistake of confronting me even though he was wanted.

Wanted for Two Years!

A description in the newspaper read, "A man wanted for rape in the first degree, for the past two years, is arrested when he picked a fight with a security officer, who was working in a local supermarket."[23]

The account is that I was working my second front in this particular market, when these two men were acting suspicious, because it appeared to me that they were casing the place. I asked them both for identification and they then jumped me. I must mention that the store personnel assisted in subduing them.

While we were waiting for a squad car to arrive, I ran a check of police department files, which disclosed that there was a warrant in effect for rape in the first degree, and it happened to be two years old and was legal to serve. (Refer to article on the liquor squad in which I arrested his father.)

* * *

A threat was made and I had to act in front of a crowd.

Remember that this was just a second job and as I have stated previously, I seemed to be in more danger working them, than on my police job, as the following story explains.

I was working my second job at a local supermarket, when a man I had never seen before came up to me and in a loud voice said, "I eat cops, for breakfast, lunch and dinner." I told him to leave the store because of the threats made to me, and it must be noted that several persons in the store had overheard this remark, so I was put in the position to take some sort of action. The man turned his back on me and appeared to comply with my wishes.

At this moment, I sensed what his next move might be, and I was right, as he spun around and tried to lay a punch directly at my jaw. My instincts came into play, and I threw him with a judo throw, which landed him on his back directly in front of me. However, it was at this moment I saw that he was reaching for a weapon hidden in his boot and I quickly kicked him in the face to defend myself from another attack.

It was only after his arrest when he screamed at me, "You're lucky! I thought I had my knife in my boot! I would have cut you, man!"

My answer was, "No, if you would have come up with a knife, I would have shot you, so it is you, my friend, who is the lucky one."

I would have been legally justified if he had come up with a knife.

* * *

The answering of a telephone just happened to land me a job as the next circumstance describes.

Necessary Second Job!

The phone rang in my office, and the manager of a factory in our precinct told me his people were being mugged going to work. He wanted someone to guard the outside of the plant at 6: 00 a.m., and he said he was aware that he could not get special attention from the patrol cars, but if I could provide someone off duty, he would pay him to stand and watch the employees as they come to work.

This was a known drug area and the junkies were always on the lookout for victims to satisfy their habit. One woman ended up beaten badly and we were unable to solve it. The attack came from behind her and she never got a look at her assailant. I listened to what he had to say and then I informed him that I would be happy to take the job myself.

My duties were to open the parking lot gate at 6:00 a.m. and close at 7:50 a.m. as the employees started their shifts. I then drove down the street to get to my police job on time. On days I couldn't make it, I hired one of the precinct detectives who took my place during my vacations, and other times I couldn't make it to this job. The muggings went down, as certain suspects would walk on by, look at me as a show of police presence, in that I wore a uniform and had a 9mm automatic strapped to my belt. There was only one challenge made to me. An individual didn't like my being there, so he decided to test me. He came up to me and had the nerve to spit in my face. A struggle ensued as I placed him under arrest. This ended the fears of the women employees of this plant who were going to work.

I stayed on this job for several years and got along great with the employees. When the plant closed to move to the suburbs, they asked me to come along and work the same job. I thanked them for their kind offer, but I explained to them that I would be unable to float between jobs the way I had been doing while I was working in their employ. The people collected some money and gave me a nice going away present, in consideration for what I had done for them. I will always remember the friends I made while working there. They were a great bunch of people to work with under the conditions in which the plant was located. It was too bad that they had to hire someone in the first place, because of the crime in that particular area, but unfortunately that's the way our society is now days.

In closing this chapter as you look back, you will see as I have mentioned before, that I was in more danger and got involved in more fights working a second job.

* * *

Follow along as we stake out an apartment at the request of a victim of burglary.

Chapter Twenty-Three
Stakeout

We interviewed a victim of a burglary, who said to us, "Can you guys stake out my apartment. You know, like the TV shows?"

"Maybe we should try it," we said to each other, only because this man had been a victim on three separate occasions. We left the immediate area and parked around the corner, in the event that someone was watching our movements. We made the trip back to the victim's house in a roundabout way, climbing over some backyard fences and doubling back so that we could reenter our man's apartment through his rear door.

The victim drove away from his apartment. Little did we know what was about to transpire in this stakeout! It was decided that my partner would hide in the bathroom, while I went into the rear bedroom closet. We had some action right away! It was only a few minutes when I heard the lock on the door turning.

To my surprise, I watched as this burglar went through the bedroom dresser drawers and took some cash. He continued to search the drawers, but he must have felt my presence, as in a sixth sense, because he turned to look in my direction. I came out of my hiding place as he started to rush out of the apartment. I yelled to my partner, "He's coming your way!" I was now in close pursuit right behind the burglar, as both of us then passed my partner in the hall, before he came completely out of the bathroom. I was still right behind the burglar, and was in the process of chasing him, when he surprised me by running upstairs and screaming to someone, "Get the shotgun." Of course, this made me run faster, because I wasn't about to be shot by the person he was yelling to. I was still in close pursuit thereby chasing him into an upstairs bathroom.

I was confronted by a naked woman, who apparently was too scared to comply with his wish to get the shotgun, which was behind the door. However, he attempted to reach for it, but he was too slow, as I had already thrown him up into the air and into the bathtub filled with hot water, which the female had drawn for her bath. He then made up a story that he really thought we were the burglars in the house below, and this is why he attempted to get the shotgun, so he could hold us at bay until the police came. We found out later, after he went to court on this matter, that he ended up evicted from the apartment that he shared with his girlfriend. We also learned that he was some kind of judo expert but I guess he lost this match to me, in that he was the one who ended up in a bathtub full of hot water! This was a good stakeout and much talked about as they usually don't work out this well!

* * *

In the next chapter follow us on the streets, as we back up the patrol force on some hot calls which they faced day in and day out, as they patrolled the streets of the city of Buffalo.

Chapter Twenty-Four
Street Patrol

The patrol force of any department are the eyes and ears of the city. It was because of our relationship with the patrolmen that we were able to receive countless pieces of information during the course of our careers. We gave credit where credit was due, and never cheated them out of any recognition, which is probably why we received several awards from the patrolmen's organization.

Some people think that detectives are supposed to stay behind a desk, or like some do, drive around with their radio off so that they won't be involved in anything. I only mentioned this because of an experience I had with an older detective who told me, when I asked why he turned the radio off, "You won't get into any trouble if you don't hear anything or never answer any calls, because that's what the patrolmen are for." His opinion, not mine!

My partner Joe and I never thought of it that way, because we always answered hot calls, making us available for backup when necessary. Ask any patrolman who knew us, because they would agree with this statement. All the police officers we had the privilege of working with on the streets of Buffalo knew this and respected us for it. They answered countless more calls than we did, along with the hot calls and the nuisance calls, whereas we could pick and choose, while they had to answer every call put to them.

We had permission from the chief of detectives at that time to do this. We were sure to inform the radio dispatcher that we were responding, so there would be no mistakes as to who we were, because of us being in plainclothes and thereby eliminating the risk of being shot by another responding officer.

The following is an example of such an occurrence.

* * *

A Dangerous Moment for Him

I responded to a call of a man with a gun, and I was startled to see a man who fit the description near me, and noted he had a revolver. I yelled to him, "Police, drop your weapon," but much to my surprise, he pulled out a badge, which was on a chain around his neck, and with this, he didn't say a word to me, but continued walking away. I don't think that he realized the dangerous situation which he had placed himself in by answering this particular call, because I could have shot him, as well as any other officer who responded. This individual should have had the courtesy to at the least say something, but he didn't.

There was a code system put out over the teletype messages, and read at roll call, to enable officers to recognize these individuals. One of the procedures, in addition to the badge, was to have a bandanna around his head, which displayed the color of the day, so that he would be easily identified as a police officer.

This particular person put himself in danger because of the simple fact that he fit the description and had no headband on when he answered the call.

* * *

In this next case I observed a man trying to hand a woman a gun, but she would not take it from him. I chased him into a known nightclub. Picture this, we seem to be playing "ring-around-the-rosie" when we ran around the tables inside. Then we went out the same door again, with me still in pursuit.

I fired a warning shot into the air,

Pow!

But this did not even faze him, because he continued running, even though cut because of crashing through the glass door of the nightclub. He kept on running down the side streets, with me still behind him. I was in plainclothes, not in uniform.

I fired another warning shot,

Pow!

He fell to the payment!

And it was at this time I said to myself, *"I couldn't have hit him as I fired straight up in the air."*

He managed to get up and the chase continued for several more blocks. He then cut down a side street in an attempt to shake me but I was still right behind him. I managed to chase him into an alley and then up some stairs. When he stumbled, I hit him on the back of the head with the butt of my gun, and tackled him, as a loaded .38 -caliber revolver flew from his bleeding hand. I lay on top of him to keep him down as I waited for my partner to catch up with me and assist in the capture.

We had to take this individual to the hospital first, because the glass in the door cut him. When we arrived there, he tried to tell the personnel at the hospital that I shot him, and then he had the nerve to flirt with the nurses while they were attending to him, by trying to make a date with one of them.

I was investigating another case several years later and I inquired about him. They told me he died.

* * *

Look! Really Look!

You have to have street smarts, and look at people and actions on the street (like the above case for instance). Some police officers say they look, but they don't see what the seasoned cop sees!

In addition, I knew a few police officers who look but pretend they don't see anything because they don't want to get involved or be accused of making a mistake.

* * *

I've been here before, were my thoughts as I answered the following call. It was like

The Twilight Zone!

We were patrolling a high-crime-rate area of the city, when we noticed a man and woman on the corner. The man was punching her in the stomach, even though she was pregnant. He continued to strike her there!

I got out of the car and yelled "Police" and went to her assistance. The assailant then ran down the street, entered a house, with me close behind him, and then into a rear bedroom. I suddenly realized it was like being in the twilight zone, because it was the same house in which I grew up, and this was my bedroom.

How do you like this for an uncanny series of events?

I am sorry to say that some years later, this particular street was named in the local newspapers as the "Killing fields" due to the number of homicides and serious assaults because of the drug problems of the people living there.

The name of the street was Box Avenue.

* * *

The Feel of the Streets

It all started when we were cruising in a particular area of the city. It must be noted that we had our windows rolled down, so that we could hear what was going on outside of our vehicle.

We were taught that in order to get the feel of the street, this is what you had to do. You had to let the windows down so that you will able to stop, look, and listen to the sounds and the smells of the street, otherwise you will never survive!

Like I mentioned before, we were looking, really looking!

But in this particular case, it wasn't what we saw, but what we heard, and if we wouldn't have had the windows down we would have never heard this.

There was a car in front of us with a woman standing next to it and she was engaged in a conversation with the driver. I overheard her say, "I don't want to touch that gun." I informed my partner on what I heard.

I got out of our car and then walked up to the driver's side of that car, where the woman was standing, and asked the driver about the gun. I stood back from the driver's window as we were taught to do, which in this particular case saved my life. I have to explain, because the driver had to turn his head to his left, and look back towards me. I have to say for sure that this did save my life because when I looked into the window he was going for his gun. I noticed that his hand casually slipped from the steering wheel to the weapon on the seat!

Now, I must admit that I was foolish, as I didn't have my gun drawn yet, but I was quick and drew it in a flash, and pointed it directly at him while he had his hand on his gun. I asked him to step from the car, and immediately took the gun from the seat. I ordered the passenger out as well, while my partner also held them at gunpoint. After I got the gun off the seat, we arrested the individuals, and then we had a problem.

The driver was a huge man, about 250 pounds, and he fought with us. A crowd gathered from the local gin mill. The driver screamed for them to get us. "Don't let them arrest us," he shouted. This was the reason someone put the call in to help us, and I have to say that we owed them a favor.

"And the beat goes on" He was reaching for his gun and I was lucky that I wasn't killed right there. I could have shot him and been justified in doing so!

* * *

In this next call we were confronted with a

Saber Attack

We answered a call of an irrational youth, and upon our arrival at the address mentioned by radio, a youth confronted us with a three-foot saber. He charged at us from the porch, causing us to draw our guns. "Put the sword down," we yelled. He then complied with our demands.

His family was having problems with him, and they were afraid of what he might do next. We advised them on what method to use with regard to the mental hygiene laws and having him committed. We arrested him and assured the family that it was best to get the attention of the courts now, rather than try to resolve this matter themselves.

* * *

In this next episode I happened to notice that a vice cop was chasing this youth down the street. I knew the officer.

I sprung into action and headed the suspect off by pulling into a driveway in his path, thereby forcing him to be at my driver's door. I leaped from the car. I didn't know that it was a gun in his hand until I grabbed it and wrestled him to the ground with it still in his grip.

This story ended up in the newspapers, which stated, "Detective Chernetsky leaped from the car and knocked the weapon from his hand." It was one of those times in life when you wonder if you took the right action. I probably should have shot him instead of disarming him, as it appeared that he was turning to fire at the officer who was chasing him.

Coulda, woulda, shoulda? Had I known right away that it was a gun he was pointing at the detective, then I really would have shot him. I would have never forgiven myself if he had shot the officer who was chasing him. I was lucky that it came out the way it did!

The officer told the media that he didn't shoot at the man for fear of hitting women and children who were in the downtown area at that time.

Some brief stories

* * *

Sometimes you answer a call but don't expect to make an arrest as quickly as we did in the following case.

In another street crime, we seized two suspects in about ten minutes, after a bakery truck driver indicated they took money from him at knifepoint. We followed the leads which were furnished by neighbors. We took the suspects into custody after tracking them down to their house. I have to mention that things don't usually happen that quickly, i.e., catching someone right away after the radio call, but in this case, as luck would have it, we were right on the mark.

* * *

Six-Year-Old Shot to Death

A caption in the paper read, "East Side man was accused in the fatal shooting of a six-year-old girl, who was outside playing on the sidewalk." It was alleged that the suspect was showing a rifle to a friend when the weapon discharged striking the little girl. When we came upon the scene, we were unaware of what had transpired. All we saw was that his man and woman were taking the girl to the hospital in their car as they sped away. We followed them to the hospital and found out that the girl had died upon arrival there. After further investigation by the homicide squad this man was charged with her death.

* * *

What do you do when confronted with the possible death of a child upon answering a shooting call? Here is another case of a child shot!

Four-Year-Old Shot Between the Eyes

We answered a shooting call and upon our arrival at this particular house, I saw a four-year old boy lying on the bed with a bullet hole in his forehead, right between the eyes. I knew the rule, don't move him, but upon looking at him, I could not wait for an ambulance to be called, and I then said to myself

He will die if I wait!

I immediately wrapped him in a blanket, cradled his head in the crook of my elbow, so as not to move his head, and immediately went outside to a patrol car, which had also responded to this call. "Go to the nearest hospital," I yelled to the officer who was behind the wheel, as I jumped in the back with the child. "Radio ahead and alert the doctors on what we were dealing with," I went on to say.

The doctors were in the driveway of the hospital when we pulled up and took him inside immediately, thereby saving his life. It must be noted that he had no brain damage.

We returned to the house to continue the questioning of the boy's grandfather. He explained to us, "There was a knock at the door. The boy answered it. Two men were there, and one of them had fired a shot, which struck the boy in the head."

The real story is that the boy was playing in the closet, found a shoe box with the gun in it, and started playing with the gun. While he was looking in the barrel he managed to fire the weapon. The bullet entered the forehead over the left eye, exiting through the top of the skull and then lodged in the ceiling. Further investigation disclosed that it was a .38-caliber gun which was recovered from a trash can inside the house. The grandfather was charged in this case, for lying and possession of the weapon. We found out later that the boy's father was in an Ohio prison and the mother was currently in jail on a prostitution charge.

I often wondered what happen to this particular boy, because I never ran across his name during my career.

Billy Kent, where are you today? Maybe someday you will read this book!

* * *

Saving of Lives
As in the above incident, I have saved some lives, and even if it were just one life, it would have been worth it, as we only pass this way but once. I would like to believe that maybe I have put a few persons on the right path, who might have been doomed to a further life of crime on the streets, or perhaps death by a violent act by someone else. This is in response to questions people ask, "Why is it that you do this job? For what? Look at the risk you take, look at the low pay you get and you sure don't get any respect!"

* * *

More Lives Saved
We answered a call of a holdup, when we spotted two men with knives that were chasing two girls down the street. We managed to disarm both of them and arrested them for the possession of switchblade knives. "We don't want to press charges," the two women exclaimed to us. They were afraid of what could happen to them later. If we hadn't come along when we did, the two girls would have been killed by these two men.

* * *

Everyone is tense when they hear the word "gun" when you arrive upon a call. In this next occasion I answered such a call. The police radio echoed with a call, "Shots fired," and we responded to it immediately along with other police units. When we arrived at the scene I spotted a man with a gun, and instantly gave chase. I fired a warning shot and yelled for him to stop.

At the same time, a marked unit had just pulled to the curb, and as the officers were getting out of their car, I warned them that the man I was now chasing was armed, by screaming just one word.

"Gun."

I continued in the chase, down a dark street, and lost him temporarily. Later on I found him hidden behind a parked car. We searched for the gun on him and he had none. Other police officers assisted me in a search in the area but we were unable to find it. We then assumed that he must have thrown the weapon to someone in the crowd that had gathered to watch the excitement. During the course of this investigation, a witness overheard someone talking on the telephone in the bar and saying to someone on the other end of the line, "Don't worry, we got the gun."

Later we learned that a bullet entered the tavern window thereby showering a patron with flying glass. This caused the assistant chief of detectives to order an investigation to determine whether it might have been one of our officers' bullets. I knew that the bullet could not have been from my weapon because I recalled that when I fired my warning shot, I made sure my gun was pointed upwards. It was later determined that other persons fired shots, but we could not establish whether the gunfire was directed at us or not.

The police evidence unit was called and dug the bullet out of the wall. It didn't belong to any of our officers.

* * *

In this next incident the police were surprised to find

Molotov Cocktails

A heading in a newspaper stated that "Police responded to a call of shots fired! They then found a six-pack of Molotov cocktails in a side yard, which were six pop bottles filled with gasoline, with cloth wicks." The paper went on to say, "The Lt. indicated Molotov cocktails were all set to be used: Alongside the incendiary devices were .22 cal cartridges."

* * *

This next story relates what can happen when you get the wrong impression on a particular incident because,

Things Are Not What They Appear to Be

I saw someone in the window of a car dealer's office that was supposed to be closed. I told my partner that there was a man on the floor in the doorway. We could see a body on the floor, covered with blood. I was closest to the door, and a man came out of this doorway. He spotted me and could see that I was a police officer, as I was in uniform, but he threw a punch at me anyway. I threw him so hard with a judo throw that when he landed on his bare back, it caused cuts from the cinders which were in the lot. I was a rookie then, and my partner exclaimed, "Wow, where did you learn to do that?"

It was at this time that we found out that the man on the floor was not dead, but cut by broken glass. This was due to a fistfight in the office and it got out of hand. The man who threw the punch was arrested for the assault on me.

* * *

It is very rare that you would be witness to a crime committed in your presence but such a thing happened to me

Witness to a Mugging!

We were patrolling a high-crime area of the city, and pulled up to this red light located by a bus stop. We couldn't believe our eyes because as we were sitting there waiting for the light to change, we happened to look in the enclosed bus stop shelter, and were amazed to see a person mugging an elderly woman, while the people in the bus stop ignored this. It was obvious that the individual was robbing her, because he had her purse in his hands and was going through it taking out her money.

I got out of the car, identified myself as a police officer, and grabbed him. He put up a fight and had to be forcibly subdued.

We talked to the elderly woman! "I don't want to press charges. I just want my money back. He didn't hurt me."

I then said to the people in the bus stop, "What's the matter with you people? What if that was your mother?" and the only response I received was a series of shoulder shrugs, as if they had no idea what happened.

Quick Shot

The headlines in the local paper indicated, "A quick shot saves the life of a police officer." The following story explains this situation.

There was an argument among several men, which erupted into a hail of gunfire, and the gunman had his weapon pointed right at the head of one of our narcotics officers. The lieutenant in charge of narcotics fired a shot and saved the detective's life because the bullet grazed the holdup man's lip, which caused the second gunman to flee.

We located his car and ended up taking him into custody at gunpoint in his apartment.

* * *

Two Flights of Stairs!

A caption in the paper read, "Detective chased a burglary suspect up two and one half flights of stairs before catching him in the attic."

It started when I answered a simple call of "Windows being broken," and responded with other cars who were in the area. I went in the alley of the address in question, and it was at that time that a woman who lived next door was motioning me to go into the house. I then saw a man in the doorway of the house and immediately entered and ended up chasing him up two and one half flights of stairs. He stashed the stuff he took in the burglary in the attic, along with the cash and the jewelry which he had in his pockets when we arrested him.

* * *

I wasn't prepared for what was about to become apparent when I answered this particular call, and in which I was about to shoot a man.

Please Don't Shoot My Daddy!

We were investigating a call of shots being fired in the fruit belt area of the city, and further investigation disclosed that a man in a van fired at another man on the street. The neighbors confirmed this story and gave us a distinctive description of the van with regard to its color and its roof style. We put it out over the police radio, but at this moment someone on the street yelled to me, "Here he comes again."

Sure enough, this same van came down the street. "Too late to take cover!" I said to myself. I was in the middle of the street, and he was upon me. There was another police car off to my right, which contained my captain, and he was a witness as to what transpired on the street, as these events unfolded.

I immediately drew my semi-automatic, as the van neared me, and I could see the window come down, and a pair of hands started to stick out from the van.

I was ready to fire at him.

A young boy of about five or six years of age was standing up behind him, with tears streaming down his cheeks, as he screamed out to me, "Please don't shoot my daddy!"

The man had put both hands outside the car window as he came to a complete stop, in anticipation of us handcuffing him. I could see that he had no weapon in his hands. What he had done was to drive back to pick up his son at a nearby school, and then returned to the scene to see what effect he had on what was going on in the area he had just left. When we searched him we could find no weapon on his person or in the vehicle; however, the victim and neighbors identified him as the same man who had fired the shots at them some five minutes earlier.

* * *

"And the beat goes on!" Forgive me for repeating this, but you don't know what you are getting into while in the so-called frying pan; "The beat is the call of the radio dispatcher, and the calls continue, and some officers die in the process."

These three police officers were killed over a period of about three months.

157

+++

+Officer I Knew Shot and Killed+

I have to tell you about a policemen friend of mine, whom I went to high school with, because he was shot and killed in the line of duty. I had just worked a special detail with him the week before he was killed.

This officer was on duty and wanted to question a man in a diner, because someone inside told him that this person had a gun. However, this same officer was in the process of putting his heavy winter coat on, and had his arms inside of the sleeve when he called to the man. The man turned around, drew his gun, and shot and killed the officer, and also shot and wounded the officer's partner. His partner then tried to return the gunfire, but unknown to him, a bullet had struck his arm, which caused him to have an unstable aim. The shooter was subsequently arrested and went to prison after trial, but he would never live to serve out his term in prison.[24]

* * *

+Another Officer Shot and Killed+

We lost another officer several months later, in a shootout with an armed holdup suspect.

This individual would enter taverns and line the customers up, in so doing taking their money. He did about 12 different tavern holdups this way using the same modus operandi. The police staked out various taverns in the hope of catching him, and in one tavern holdup, he managed to escape any police search, because this particular tavern did not have any officers inside.

Two officers were searching for him in the area of the holdup and were checking various taverns along the way. But when they entered this particular tavern, they asked the bartender if a man answering the description of the holdup man had entered. The bartender said, "No." But what he failed to tell the officers was that the holdup man did enter and changed clothes in a phone booth.

Just as these officers were about to leave, one of the officers thought something looked suspicious about this man who was now seated at the bar. When he confronted him, this man ended up grabbing a patron, using him as a human shield, and as he backed out the bar, he shot at the officers. One of these two officers had his hat grazed by a bullet in the gun battle which followed.[25]

There was another hail of bullets, and a patrol car answered the call of "Shots fired in a tavern," but they were unaware of the holdup, which had occurred in another adjoining precinct, and it was when they exited their police car, that one officer gave chase and followed this man around the side of the tavern.

It was dark outside! It was at this time that the holdup man fired over his shoulder, without even looking, and shot this officer right between the eyes, thus killing him instantly. The officers who were involved in the gunfight inside the tavern now came out the back door, and the gunfight continued, and the holdup man was shot and killed by them

+And Yet Another One of Our Officers Shot and Killed! +

A suspicious man was hanging around the precinct house. Several changes of shift personnel ignored him. One shift did take note of him and his behavior. A car crew attempted to take him to the hospital for observation. However, the handcuffs were placed in front of the man, not in the back. While seated in the back seat, the suspect saw that the officer slid in alongside him, but in so doing, backed into the seat. This gave the suspect an opportunity to grab this officer's gun and when he did, he shot and killed the officer who was in the front seat!

So ends the section on street patrol. So how do they cope with all this violence on the job? Some don't and they take their own life as is indicated in the next chapter.

Chapter Twenty-Five
+Suicide+

Police officers have a very high suicide rate according to a study made in a comparison with other professions. I knew some of them who took their own life for whatever reason. The following stories will tell how these officers decided not to cope with life anymore.

+++

A police officer called 911, and told the dispatcher that he was going to kill himself. Various police units responded to this call. When they arrived, they attempted to enter the house through the front door. I went to the rear. I was only there a minute when a man ran out the door and started to choke me. Naturally, I figured that this had to be the officer who called for help, and I didn't want to overreact by hurting him, so I maced him instead. Other officers then came to my assistance and they helped me subdue him. He was taken to the hospital where he could get the help he obviously needed.

+++

In this next story, a police officer had a fight with his girlfriend, and as a result of this argument, she broke up with him. This left him in a very depressed state. He felt that there was no hope of ever getting back with her.

The results were fatal, because he shot himself with his service revolver.

I knew him before he came on the force because he was a witness in a robbery case I had.

+++

A motorcycle officer took his own life at his locker because he was ill with cancer and didn't want to suffer. So, he took out his service revolver and shot himself in front of his fellow officers.

+++

Another officer was despondent over his marriage, because he felt that things were not going right. He was under the impression that his wife was cheating on him. He was wrong and no one knows what he based his feelings on.

Obviously, the police department took his gun away from him; however, he went to one of the large department stores, purchased a rifle, and then went out to his boat and shot himself.

I remembered that he used to tell one-line jokes all the time because of being a happy-go-lucky type of individual who would cheer people up with his sense of humor.

+++

There was another occurrence in the detective bureau, when a certain detective was late for work, and his associates wondered where he was. When they called his home, his wife said, "He left for work! Isn't he there?"

A check of the police garage showed that he took an unmarked car and was apparently on the move somewhere. A call to the police radio dispatcher came about in an attempt to contact him. There was no response to the radio calls that went to his vehicle. There was a search of various locations which he frequented, but this proved to be without success.

I am sorry to say that after various units made an extensive search for him, they then found his body up on some railroad tracks. It appeared that he had driven his police car there, took off his suit coat, laid it neatly next to him, and then shot himself with his service revolver. He was not ill, not in debt, and had no martial problems. It still remains a mystery to this date on why he chose to kill himself.

+++

In January of 2004, a detective friend of mine took his own life with his service revolver. He was still on the department. He was a decent man, with whom I had the pleasure of working with for several years before my retirement from police work.

+++

I am sorry to say that in December of 2004 another young police officer took his own life by shooting himself with his service revolver. I had the privilege of knowing his father, who happened to still be on the police force when this tragic event unfolded in their lives.

* * *

September 1, 2007. Unfortunately another police officer I knew killed himself with his service revolver. He used to work out with me at the Aquatic Center. He happened to be 49 years of age. Again no one knows why.

* * *

I would be the first to admit that I am not qualified to give an expert opinion on this matter, and I would venture to say that perhaps it is the easy access to a firearm which may have contributed somewhat to these types of situations. Simply because the gun is always there, and their line of reasoning is distorted, and once you pull that trigger there is no going back.

There are counseling services in place, to reach out to all officers who are depressed and need help; however, their macho image prevents them from taking this help, because of fear that they will be labeled, or have a stigma which they feel that they can't erase.

* * *

In the next story, I will explain to you a situation in which a person was so hopeless that he wanted to kill himself but did not have the nerve to do it. However, little did I know that I was about to become a victim of this individual's plot to do himself in, with regard to a call I answered.

Suicide by Police

My partner and I answered a call of a man with a gun at a busy downtown intersection. We saw a well-dressed man standing on the same corner which went out over the police radio. As I got out of the police car I said to my partner, "That's probably the guy who called about the gun," and walked over to him. As I identified myself, I remarked, "Are you the person who called the police?" I wanted him to know who I was, because I was in plainclothes. It was necessary to take out my badge and direct his attention to it to establish my identity.

I saw the gun in his waistband, and it was at that moment I realized the danger I was in. My defense mechanisms kicked in! It dawned on me what was about to become clear. I want you to know that I could feel my skin crawl, because I knew that he was about to shoot me! I was too close to him to draw my own weapon, so the only thing that I could do at this time was to grab his arms and pin them to his sides, thereby preventing him from drawing his gun.

It was at moment that my partner realized what was happening to me and immediately jumped out of the car to assist me in disarming him.

"I want to die!" this individual screamed out. "I wanted the police to kill me because I didn't have the nerve to do it myself!" It was his intention to put this fake call in, and when the police responded to it, he would shoot the first uniformed officer who answered the call. In the process, his death would come about by being killed in the ensuing gun battle with other officers.

We then realized that we saved a uniformed officer's life by being lucky enough to respond to this call first. The fact that we were in plainclothes managed to confuse him and messed up his plans.

The next chapter relates to the undercover squad on investigations related to vice charges, the so-called "victimless crimes."

Are they? You decide!

Chapter Twenty-Six
Vice

The word "vice" is in the dictionary as: "Moral depravity, or corruption."

Vice, liquor and gambling are referred to as "victimless crimes!" But aren't all these people victims too? Or do we write them off because we can't or won't see that side of the coin? In the New York State Penal Law, you will find that there are elements of what we call "vice" which are there to be enforced. There are people who have a problem with this, because they feel there should be no prosecution at all. "Who is at risk?" I ask you. Is it:
the girls who work the trade, with
the possibility
of being murdered,
or a beating by their pimps,
or by a "john,"
or becoming hooked on heroin,
because this is their excuse to forget what they are doing to their bodies.
The johns, themselves, may end up
being robbed,
or beaten,
or killed for their money,
or bring home a disease to their wife or girlfriend.

While doing this type of work, you have to try to get into various suspected houses of prostitution which were operating in certain sections of the city. Do you have to undress while doing this job, or neck with them? The answer is "No." If you do any of this, it is called entrapment. Moreover you just have to get them to say the right thing about what they are going to do for you relative to the sex act and they have to set a price for their services.

Ploys

I remember when I first started on the vice squad I was informed by more seasoned members of the squad, to be aware of the following ploys used by hookers and their pimps.

They have the John put his pants on a chair. While he is busy with the girl, her man is under the bed, taking the John's money and credit cards. The John is none the wiser, until after he leaves.

A man bursts into the room and yells, "What are you doing with my wife." He shakes the man down for money, and threatens to call his wife, knowing that this guy is not going to complain.

The John thinks he is safe because he left his wallet in the car. He then enters the house while the pimp goes through his car, while the John is busy with the girl.

* * *

Wrong Foot

How did my first assignment go? Well, listen to this conversation between me and the hooker in question. I was trying to gain access into this house of prostitution, and was at the door, asking for the woman. "Is M at home?" I asked.

The woman who answered my knock took one look at me, gazed down to my feet, and remarked, "The first thing you have to learn, Officer, is to change your shoes." I looked down and noticed that I had on my black uniform shoes, even though I was dressed in work clothes. *How's that for starting off on the wrong foot!*

* * *

The Eyes and Ears of Neighborhoods

There were complaints from the local block clubs about prostitution activity in this one particular area of the city. We set up an observation post. It was only a short time when we noticed a prostitute flag an individual down, enter his car and drive away. They went several blocks before he pulled over into a darkened alleyway. We followed them and when they stopped I tried to move into position, to see if we could possibly catch them in the act and bust them for engaging in the crime of prostitution. I made my move, which was to reach inside the car to shut off his motor. I yelled "Police" but at the same time Murphy's Law came into play, because the suspect threw the car into reverse gear, thereby catching me in the door.[26] I ran backwards as fast as I could to avoid being caught underneath the vehicle. I threw myself to the ground and rolled off to the side.

My partner could have fired a shot at the moving car as it sped away, but he didn't. There would have been justification because the suspect had almost killed me, but he held his fire because of the girl inside the moving vehicle.

* * *

In another vice case I was in a car with two suspects when unfortunately they noticed the police tail on them. I already had enough on them, and waited for the right moment to pull my badge and arrest them. It was to have been when my backup pulls them over.

Oops, Murphy's Law again!

"We'll lose those cops," the driver said, and he immediately speeded up the car in an attempt to escape. I was in the back seat. It was wintertime! There was no traffic near us, nor any pedestrians on the street. I flashed my badge and yelled, "I am a police officer! You are both under arrest." At this instant I grabbed the driver by the throat with my left arm and tried to hang on to the passenger with my right arm. He banged my wrist into the doorframe in an attempt to try to release my grip on him. Just then the car slid across the street and slammed into a pole. (Remember I was in the back seat.) At that exact moment my backup pulled up and came to my assistance.

* * *

In another assignment, I was working undercover in a bus station looking for persons who work the tourist crowd when I saw a border patrol agent but

I Thought He Knew Me!

He asked me why I was in the terminal. I responded with "I just wanted to hang around!" I was wrong! I guess this was not a good thing to say, because he pulled his gun and asked me to put my hands up, and made me go up against the wall with my feet spread eagle, while he made an attempt to search me.

It was my belief at that time, that his trained eye caught the bulge of my weapon and he was being cautious, so I had to quickly tell him that my badge was in my left pocket, and where my gun was.

* * *

In this most unusual undercover operation

I Was Asked to Commit a Crime!

I was in this same bus stations when a man, whom I didn't know, approached me and said to me, "Do you want to help me mug somebody? We could mug the next person who comes down the street!"

My answer was, "I'll go along with it, but I have to go to the bathroom first." Actually it was an opportunity for me to speak to my backup. I managed to inform my partner on what was about to transpire and told him to make sure that he would be the next man to come down the street. I quickly returned to this guy and assumed my position in front of the terminal.

Now as my partner came down the street, the man then said to me, without any encouragement from me, "Let's get this guy," and with this he then jumps my partner. But he is now jumped by me while I said to him, "We are the police, and you, my friend, are now under arrest."

Actually this worked out well because if my cover wouldn't have come down the street as we planned, some innocent civilian would have been jumped first, and may have gotten hurt in the process.

* * *

In another incident, my partner and I gained entrance to this house of prostitution! A problem arose because the girls were hesitant to commit themselves at this time. I had previously hidden my gun in a wash basket in the front room, because I knew that we might be searched. So, when this one girl came up to me she said, "I have to see if you are the police, or if you are carrying a gun. I will have to search you." With this she felt around my waistband and back. She was unable to find one and figured it was okay, because I was unarmed.

We obtained enough information to arrest them, but just then several men burst into the apartment and I thought that it was a setup. *"They were going to rob us,"* I said to myself. Before we identified ourselves, I threw myself to the floor, rolled over to the wash basket, and got my weapon out.

We took the girls in and received no problem from the two men.

* * *

Do you know what a call girl operation is? Listen to the following story about when we busted one such operation. We called an escort service, and they told us a girl would meet us wherever we wanted. We suggested a certain downtown hotel.

It wasn't too long before a young, attractive, well-groomed girl showed up. She started to take off her clothes, and as she did so, she thrust her breasts outward for us to examine. As she started to take off her underwear, we asked her the usual questions; on how much it will cost us and what she will do for us. She said, "You got a look at the goods. How much do you think I am worth?" Then she named the price and what she will do for us with regard to sex. We then arrested her on vice charges.

After we arrested her we called the escort service again. "Your girl didn't show up," we told the man who answered the phone. He gave us his name and was mad because we might have been inconvenienced, and he stated to us, "I'll send my wife. That way we'll know she will show up."

True to his word, his wife shows up, and she was also an attractive woman who looked like she didn't have to be in this business. Before anything could be said, she started this dance and took off her blouse, took off her bra, and then told us what we wanted to hear before disrobing any further. We stopped her there because we had the necessary information, and arrested her.

We went to the escort bureau and arrested her husband, which resulted in us shutting down this escort service.

* * *

They aren't all street walkers. Let me tell you about this other case when we attempted to arrest a woman who was using a call girl operation. We arranged a meet with her in a downtown hotel. She showed up and engaged us in a conversation relative to what she was going to do for us with regard to sex, and how much it will cost us.

It was when she started to take off her clothes that we quickly arrested her on the charge of prostitution. She became very upset with us and said, "I deserve some respect! I'm not a common gutter tramp, like some other women. I am a high-class girl, not a common street walker."

It was later determined that she had some $50,000 in a secret bank account, which her husband was not aware of, nor was he aware of her second job ventures either. Now you have to admit that she had this great background which consisted of money and had a high-class home in the suburbs, but in our eyes, this still made her no better than a common streetwalker.

* * *

In this particular case I found myself in an only-one-of-its-kind situation.

Man in Drag!

I attempted to arrest this man for soliciting and he was in complete female attire! When I arrested him he put up a struggle and I had to fight with him before my backup got to me. We were on a crowded street and he screamed "Rape," but before the crowd could assist him, I pulled off his blouse and I pulled off his brassiere, in an attempt to show the crowd that he was in fact a man and there was no rape in progress. This satisfied the people who tried to help him.

I have to tell you that he wore his complete outfit when we went to court, because he had nothing else to wear. His attorney took him to the bench, dressed the way he was, and pled him guilty. He took his money, or whatever else he could get for collateral from this man.

Now I ask you, who are the real victims here? This same lawyer had a problem with this one particular judge, in that he always told the judge that he had an engagement in another part of the court and would never come right back as ordered to do by this judge.

On several occasions, the judge ordered the bailiff to handcuff him to the front rail so as to be sure that he would be available. We nicknamed him "Fat Stuff" from the *Smiling Jack* comic strip, because he looked like him, and his buttons would be popping off his shirt while in the courtroom, which was the same as the cartoon character.

* * *

During the course of this next investigation I was confronted with the dangers of the job when I thought she was unarmed, but

I Could Have Lost an Eyeball!

There was an occasion in which I pulled my badge, as I was taught to do, and immediately slapped the cuffs on this hooker, whom I had picked up in my own private vehicle. (I must explain sometimes we had to use our own vehicles in some of these prostitution arrests!)

I asked her for her knife, as they always carried protection against the street johns. She said "Okay" and handed me a razor blade, which was between her fingers! I must admit, I didn't see it! I was glad that she didn't resist arrest, because if she would have turned and slapped me across the face with this razor, I would have been looking out a new eyeball!

* * *

In this next case one defendant who was testifying in court stated an occasion describing when

My Backup Entered with a Bang!

There was testimony going on in court, when one of the witnesses for our defendant starting ranting and raving while on the stand. He complained that

170

my backup knocked on the door, and before he could completely open it, the door was knocked off its hinges. He was pinned under the door, when this huge man charged in, stepped on the door, while he was under it, and continued up the stairs.

This was my cover, and he is a huge man, but the witness lied because he really was trying to hold the door shut while I was in trouble on an arrest upstairs.

* * *

In the next series of stories I want to explain unusual sets of circumstances when an undercover operative by the name of Ray had all

Bad Luck!

The reason I am mentioning these events, is that in an unusually short time, this detective known to us as "Ray" was the victim of repeated attacks on his person, which was against the law of averages.

In one instance, he tried to pick up a hooker in his own vehicle and was having a conversation with her. It was at this time that her pimp came up and sprayed Ray in the face, with a noxious spray! (His window was down!) We rushed Ray to the hospital to get his eyes washed out.

There was another situation when we were in the downtown theatre district, because of numerous complaints of lewd activity in the men's room. It was the job of the vice squad to investigate these complaints and act on them.

Ray was in this small bathroom alone, when a guy came in, looked at him, recognized him as an undercover officer, and then threw a large cherry bomb into the bathroom.

Ray suffered ear damage from this attack.

Doesn't everyone carry one with him when going to the bathroom?

In still another happening, he picked up a hooker and went to her place, and we were supposed to be following him, but lost him in traffic. When we searched for him, we were able to spot his vehicle in the rear of a suspected house of prostitution. We ended up at the back staircase to the house, when we heard a large crash, and there was Ray, being thrown through a large window, by a husky woman.

171

I entered the house, and she said, "Don't hit me, I'm a lady."

My response was, "After I saw what you just did to my partner, you're no lady." She tried to punch it out with me, and a struggle ensued but it was no contest as she was subsequently subdued and placed under arrest for the assault on Ray.

In yet another unpleasant episode, there was a heading in the paper, which said, "OSI *(OSI then stood for Office of Special Intelligence.)* Undercover agent is in emergency hospital, after being kicked in the stomach, while on the arrest of a suspect who was sold him hot rings."

Of course, you guessed it, they were referring to Ray.

* * *

Women are not even safe in their homes when it comes to a

Phone Stalker!

In this case, a telephone pest bothered a local housewife. It appeared that this man seemed to be watching her movements, as he knew when she came in her house and when she went out. He asked her personal questions with regard to what she wore and then he went into conversations about her sex life, on what she liked and didn't like.

He wanted to meet her somewhere. We told her to go along with it and she then set up an arrangement to meet in a local theater which was nearby. He fell for it and showed up at the theater, sat next to her, and at this point, he engaged her in a conversation.

We had previously advised her to make sure he is the same man who talked to her on the phone. We did this, because it could have been some other spook who tried to make out with her, because of the fact she was a female and seated by herself. We told her to give us a high sign, if she is sure he is our suspect, and sure enough it was the right man, because she did what we told her, which enabled us to take him into custody. We had the assistance of two other detectives who we had sat close by, because we didn't want to take a chance of something happening to her.

It was found out later that this individual was a neighbor who lived close by, who had watched her come and go out of her house for quite a while before he actually got the nerve up to call her on the phone.

* * *

Earlier in this chapter I had mentioned victims. Listen to this bust! I was about to arrest a prostitute when she was in the process of shooting up with heroin in my presence. But before I could stop her, she already had the needle stuck in her arm. I put her under arrest and she said to me, with tears in her eyes, "I'm sorry; I have to give myself a shot first."

We added the charge for instruments to administer narcotics, as well as the prostitution charge. Perhaps she can get some help with her addiction.

* * *

Waiting to Be Mugged!

I was still on the undercover squad, and had put myself in a position to be mugged. We had complaints of muggings in this particular area. Four men engaged me in a conversation, and attempted to lure me into an alley near this hotel, because I would then be out of sight of anyone who might pass by.

My backup wasn't close enough. I saw that I was about to take a beating, so I immediately identified myself as a police officer. They continued their attack. One of them attempted to kick me in the crotch, just grazing my inseam! I immediately pulled my gun and fired a shot in the air. It was at that time that my backup came to my assistance and we arrested the four of them.

It was the first time I had fired my gun in self-defense!

* * *

In this next episode we were responding to a tip that they were having obscene shows in this local tavern which was located in a decent neighborhood.

The bar was a local pit stop, which didn't look like much from the outside. We had complaints from the neighbors because there seem to be a lot of activity there and someone wrote, "They have sex on top of the bar."

It took a few trips to check the place out because my partner and I could only go in there occasionally, because we had other investigations we were responsible for. It appeared that nothing was going to happen. There were always a lot of patrons when we went in there. They appeared to be from all over the city though, not just from this particular neighborhood. The owner eyed me suspiciously even though I always engaged him in a conversation. He just didn't trust me at this time. When we thought that something might happen he would then clam up. This was especially when someone asked him when is there going to be another show, to which he didn't answer but eyed me nervously.

One day, I ran into him at the downtown YMCA because I belonged to the Buffalo Judo club. I was lifting weights while he engaged me in a conversation. I told him I fought in sport judo matches across the state. (Which I really did!) "Where do you work?" he asked.

"I work for the city" was my answer.

The next time I came into his bar, I noticed that the mood was more relaxed. He dimmed the lights. One of his bartenders passed a tray around and collected money for a show. I put money in too! A young male patron put the number seven flag up over the bar. I knew what it meant, as I served a tour of duty in the Navy. It meant, "Look out, diver below," because it was a warning to ships who passed by. It had the same meaning here, i.e. diver below, but with different connotations, as you can well imagine, with regard to sex under the number seven flag!

The owner locked the front door and secured the blinds. I looked around and noticed there appeared to be about 100 patrons inside the bar. Just then a scantily clad, attractive woman climbed up on the bar and did a dance to which everyone applauded. They knew what was about to happen, as she then took off all her clothes and lay down on the bar beneath the number seven flag.

A young man with no shirt then came up to the bar and did a few dance steps. He then performed oral sex on the young lady. At that moment, I yelled, "Police, this is a raid!"

I held my badge in my left hand up high for everyone to see, and then with my right hand, I grabbed the young man by the nape of the neck and pulled him out from between her legs. It was at this time I flung him across the bar to get him out of the way. He turned around and yelled to me, "I'm not doing anything wrong why pick on me?"

I immediately unlocked the front door to let the rest of our squad in. My partner showed his badge and blocked the rear exit which kept all the patrons from leaving.

Crowds at the Trial!

Now, the trial, that was another matter entirely! It was a great spectacle on the court circuit. In the press reports, the judge refused to permit any further delays, and ordered the selection of the jury to start the next day. Police said they were opposed to this because the girl was in the Western Reformatory for Women, on another matter. She had to come here under guard and was lodged in the county jail.

A tactic by a defense attorney was that he wanted to adjourn because a story in the local paper was prejudicial to his female client.

The trial was then set down to be held on December 16, 1964.

On February 4, 1965, the motion was denied for the mistrial of the three in the tavern case. A local paper wrote, "A Detective testified, about the dance, and he indicated that patrons contributed cash, for the show. The police department stated that he checked out the tavern in advance." (The detective was me!)

The vice trial had to be moved to a larger room, because the judge wanted the move to prevent the jury, a panel of five men and one woman, from being distracted by the constant traffic flow of spectators. This caused him to order the court detail to be on hand to maintain order among the number of spectators.

The judge denied their motion for a mistrial. Here are some other comments made by the defense attorneys in their attempt to sway the jury during the trial.

They indicated that it was I who banged on the bar and screamed, "Bring on the show," and they said that I started the money tray around and was the first person to put money into it.

They also said that I should have not allowed this to happen and was responsible for her being violated, and should have stopped the act sooner that I did.

The girl was charged with indecent exposure and attempted sodomy, while the owner was charged with disorderly premises and abetting an indecent show.

The young man ended up charged with attempted sodomy. The owner alleged that he went to the back room for supplies, and didn't know what was happening in the front of the tavern.

On February 10, 1965, the judge said the jury needed funds for meals.

The tavern operator, who was 25 years of age, and the woman, who was 18 years of age, who was the daughter of a Rochester dentist, ended up convicted in this case.

The third defendant, the young man, who was 22 years of age, ended up acquitted on the morals charge because the jury could not believe that he could do this crime while sober.

Friends of his had testified that he was in several other taverns before coming here, which caused the jury to indicate that they thought that he would have to be drunk to do this act in front of 100 people. I testified that he was not drunk, and that he knew what he was doing.

Young Girl Pays with Jail Time!

Others go free!

The tavern owner ended up on probation and paid a small fine. The girl went to prison for some three and one half years because she had other charges pending.

Note: This case could have been a book in itself as was suggested by some attorneys who were privy to the information.

Now, I ask you the reader, who are the real victims in these vice cases?

Is it the young girl who did jail time?

Or, the real villain who set it up?

Or, the man who performed sex on her body?

Or, the girl who gave herself a shot before sex?

Or, the man in drag?

Or, the john who was killed?

Or, is it Ray, who was hurt and could have been killed?

So you see, there are many victims in this so-called victimless crime!

* * *

Liquor Squad

Did you have a good time at an illegal party? There are liquor laws that are on the books to be enforced, but the public does not think they should be there at all. In their point of view these laws are nothing but a waste of taxpayers' time and money to have this in the court system!

Have you ever been to a speakeasy, where they are not licensed to serve liquor, or to an after-hours establishment where they serve liquor beyond the legal hour? Well that's what we are talking about!

These stories are relative to investigations, for a short time, which occurred while I was in the process of trying to enforce the liquor laws according to the State Liquor authority's ABC laws. (Alcohol, Beverage, and Control).

You think that you are doing a good job and that you are not made as a cop when someone whispers in your ear

Psst! We Know Who You Are!

I was in this tavern near closing time, and in the process of obtaining drinks with no problem. I guess it was my imagination at first, because I felt that they waited for me to leave. I was right, because a few minutes later after I had gone to the phone to tell my backup people that I might be able to make this place, a man came up to me and said, "Tell them that you are not going to bring this place down because we know who you are."

Of course, I didn't leave right away, but stayed a little while longer to make it look good, because I wanted them to think that they made a mistake in their assumption that I was an undercover operative.

* * *

In this instance you think that you are cool but in fact you are not dressed for the place you are in and you

Stuck Out Like a Sore Thumb

There was another situation when I was in a tavern. You have to dress for the area that you work. I sure wasn't ready for what was about to take place while inside.

I was in there to check on minors being served, but I didn't wear the right clothes for the type of place I was in, and noticed that the crowd was a little unfriendly, as they demonstrated their disapproval of the war in Vietnam, because of news on the TV. Just then a young lady came up to me and said, "I don't know who you are, but they think that you are a cop and intend to jump you when you go out the door, and take your gun away from you."

There was another agent in the bar. I signaled for him to go to the bathroom where I had a brief discussion with him and informed him of what the young girl told me. I then told him to alert the squad to what had transpired and move up closer as backup, and perhaps, witness them attack me when I went outside.

You really do not think of the danger at that time. Now that I look back, I recalled saying that. I was just a rookie then.

I positioned myself with my back against the bar. I think they wanted to test my reaction, because a gang member came up to me, smashed a beer bottle, and held it by the neck, as if he was going to cut me. In the meantime, another person asked me what I thought of the war, and tried to paste a protest sticker on my forehead, but I sidestepped him. I had my gun in the small of my back, and watched the man with the beer bottle and thought about my next move, as I said to myself: *"I might have to shoot this man in self-defense."*

The crowd chanted to the TV set, "Johnson get the troops out of Vietnam now." I didn't want to blow my cover, and held my position! The two persons who confronted me backed off and joined the crowd.

I left the bar thinking what the girl had said to me. No one made a move to follow me outside. It was my opinion that they must have known something was up.

A few months later, I arrested this same man who had put the bottle to me, but this was in relation to another incident; however, before he went to trial, he died in a gunfight with a rival gang member.

* * *

In yet another experience, the newspapers wrote an article about a speakeasy in which they stated that "100 patrons went to the street, with four persons arrested, after Central Investigation Bureau police *(liquor squad)* raided three suspected speakeasies in scattered parts of the city early today." The chief of detectives stated that the patrons were mostly "Show people and other regular nightlife's, favoring illegal liquor spots." They had a periscope-type lookout mechanism behind a blower. The furnished apartment had paintings on the walls, along with sofas and overstuffed chairs. There was a mahogany bar along with soft lights and a hi-fi set playing. A weapons charge was placed against the owner of the premises, but little did I know that some years later, I would end up making an arrest of this man's son on an old warrant.[27]

* * *

We Were Searched at the Door

While in the process of a raid of another speakeasy, we were stopped at the entrance by a guard who informed us that he would have to check us for weapons in the event that we were the police. It was at this time that he frisked my partner and felt his gun, which caused my partner to pull it out and say, "Does this look like a police gun to you? I carry this gun for protection." The gun was an automatic which were not common to the police at that time, so the guard replied "No" and allowed us to enter the premises without any more fuss. We ended up with several arrests there and to add a point of humor, all we heard from the guard then were his words, over and over, "I sure am stupid. I sure am stupid."

So, the next time you are in an after-hour place think of what happens if the police should raid the premises and you are one of those being booked, or maybe you become a witness to something or your name ends up in the paper.

Gambling

Do you place a two-dollar bet? Do you go to the track? We all gamble at one time or another, whether it's the two-dollar bet at the track, or lottery, or bingo, or other forms of gambling. Some aspects of gambling are on the books as a crime and law enforcement officers have to enforce them, even though some of the public does not like it. These stories are about cases which I was involved in while I was on the gambling squad, but it was only for a very short time, because I was then switched to the vice squad. My assignment on the gambling squad was after I was out of the precinct for only a year, and I was put there because they needed a new face.

* * *

In yet another situation, I was in an area known for bookmaking operations. In so doing, I watched persons who wrote up bets on the street. I was doing surveillance on this one man who spoke to several people on the street, and I noticed that he looked in my direction and then threw a slip of paper down on the sidewalk and walked away quickly. I went across the street and bent down while pretending to tie my shoe. I obtained the slip of paper, read it, but out of sight of the man on the corner, and noted that written on the paper was one word

"Gotcha!"

I then walked away slowly. I was embarrassed about this strategy he pulled on me to ascertain whether or not I was an operative. But it worked!

* * *

Mothers and Grandmothers Are Holy, or Are They?

I was on a raid of a house suspected of a large bookmaking operation, in which we then obtained all the evidence we needed: i.e. bets, flash paper, etc.

The man who was arrested said that we couldn't arrest him as he didn't own the house, and whined to us, "Don't take me, take my mother, she owns this house." If you can picture this in your mind, he was a husky man, while she was a frail old woman, and he didn't care one way or another what happened to her, as long as he was a free man.

These crimes are still on the books and the general public is at odds on how to deal with them in the courtroom and in their own personal lives. So, the next time you place your bet or go to the track think about just where that money really goes. Victims have lost their homes and families due to overdoing the gambling bit.

* * *

I was on this particular squad (i.e., vice, liquor & gambling) for three and one half years, until I finally obtained my transfer to the robbery squad.

Now follow along for the rest of the stories in the next few; pages as my career winds down.

Now, for the Rest of the Story!

September 2, 1994

I thought that I would obtain a serious injury or be killed on this job before my career was finished, but none of that happened. But what did happen is that I came down with a serious illness.

Let me explain the situation to you, as to what transpired on that particular day in my life, which changed it forever.

I was about to take my two younger daughters to the hairdresser, and I didn't feel too well, but couldn't put my finger on it. All I felt at that time was stomach cramps, so I drove them there. I was at the hairdresser when one of the women there said to me, "You don't look right, Mike. Are you okay? Why don't you leave the girls here, and we will get you a ride home." One of the women there then drove me home.

We arrived at my house just as my wife pulled up. It was at that time that I started to get more pains in my stomach. My wife assisted the woman from the hairdresser in getting me out of the car. I refused to go to the hospital and went upstairs to bed. I was in bed for about an hour and the pain in my stomach persisted. I then recalled what my mother, who was an immigrant, always said, "If you go to the hospital, make sure you have clean underwear on!" I yelled down to my wife, as a joke, "I'm putting on clean underwear; take me to the hospital."

I am supposed to know first aid, and know the symptoms of a heart attack; however, I was in for a surprise of my life, when they told my wife at the hospital that I had suffered a bad heart attack.

I was treated and stayed at the hospital for a while and at that time, a heart doctor then recommended that I take a stress test. I thought I did well! I was then informed that I needed heart surgery and then ended up having a triple bypass surgery, and am lucky to be writing this, because it was a blessing in disguise, since my arteries were blocked, I was overweight, had high cholesterol, and a high-stress job.

I was told that I could die if I did not have this surgery.

I remember the day well, because on November 14, 1994, I had triple bypass surgery at Millard Fillmore Hospital in Buffalo, New York.

Another day I remembered well was on December 14, when I had a stroke at home! At that time I collapsed to the floor and felt the whole left side of my body go limp, from my arm down to my leg. I want to say that I was fortunate that my stepdaughter, Amy, was home at the time, so when I yelled downstairs for her to call 911, she readily did so.

I took my nitro tablets at that time, but the rescue squad informed me later that I shouldn't have taken them, because they were just for a heart attack as they lowered my blood pressure.

I still had my sense of humor however and remember saying to them, "Whatever you do don't give me CPR, as I had my chest sawed open in my heart bypass operation." I went to the hospital, and again I was fortunate, as my paralysis lasted for about five hours and at that time, I regained the full use of my left side. I know that I was very fortunate!

Thank God that I survived this latest ordeal, because prior to this, as I lay there on the floor, my whole life seemed to flash before me, as I thought that perhaps it was coming to an end.

(Thanks to the good work of the Tonawanda Rescue Squad and the Kenmore Police.)

Epilogue

"It ain't over until it's over," said the Yankee great, Yogi Berra.

However, it was over for me. I returned to the streets of Buffalo after being off sick with a serious illness for six months. I had a heart attack, heart surgery, and a stroke

I was only on the streets for one tour of duty when I realized that a punch in the stomach or in the chest would put my life in danger.

I decided to turn in my badge and gun, after I served some 34 years on the police department.

I know that I left the city in good hands, with the great people "who are behind this badge" and are out there walking this thin blue line, by just serving the community the best way they know how.

I retired from the Buffalo Police Department on March 17, 1995. I used to make sure that I had my gun and cuffs on before I left the house; now I check to see if have my nitro and other medicines on me before I go out.

The Aquatic and Fitness Center
My Road to Recovery!

I wasn't working the streets as a detective in Buffalo anymore, and was in the process of recovering from my illness of a heart attack, heart surgery and a stroke.

In October of 1995, I joined a gym by the name of the Aquatic and Fitness Center located in the town of Tonawanda, NY. I was in the process of trying to regain my health here.

I was lucky to find fine instructors there, like Sheila[28], who first trained me on the proper use of equipment. I found all the trainers to be patient with the elderly and persons recovering from an illness.

I used the weights, the rowing machine, the treadmill, and other cardio equipment. It was tedious at first, but over time I managed to regain my strength by gradually increasing my workout routine on the various machines, particularly on the treadmill and on the rowing machine.

I also made full use of the pool, as well as the hot tub, but in moderation. There were some other members who had the same kind of problems as I did. I encouraged the new ones who just had a heart attack recently. I said to Sheila, "Some of the guys are trying to copy my exact routine but I advised them to go in moderation."

She said, "That was the right answer to give them."

The atmosphere was friendly and I enjoyed talking with various individuals who worked out there. I wasn't the only one with this outlook.

The oldest person I met there was a gentleman named Tony who is 92. He told me, "I enjoy it here. I have a bus for seniors which drops me here in the morning and picks me up in the afternoon."

Another man on the rowing machine had once told me, "I enjoy the people. I come here and do my thing, but I really like the company here."

Some persons work out on Monday, Wednesday and Friday, while others work out on Tuesday, Thursday, and Saturday. Only by working out every day will you meet them all. In the past few years they have added TV's, so the persons on the bikes and treadmills can watch it. These are in captions and I found out that most regulars are concerned with watching the news, and then discussing it with others.

I also want to mention that I came across various coincidences, some of which were eerie.

First and foremost, I ran into an officer who first broke me in on the police department, Ralph Archibald[29]. I spoke with him on a daily basis and we talked of the old days when he broke me in as a rookie cop in precinct #15. He always had a smile on his face. He wore an oxygen tank, as he had trouble breathing at times, but never complained about it.

I reacquainted myself with another police officer, Jim Weiser, who is a retired detective sergeant from the fraud squad. I have to tell you that I had the privilege of knowing his father, Detective Sergeant Gene Weiser, who was the head of the evidence unit at one time. Jim's grandfather, Albert Weiser, was a motorcycle officer who died in 1939.

I also ran into a friend, Tony Constantino, who is a retired detective sergeant from Buffalo's elite homicide squad. Likewise, we talked over old times about some of the cases we worked on together. It went "remember when " or "remember that occasion." His son Mark is a police officer working in a high-crime area in Buffalo, while his daughter Lora is a federal customs officer.

I met George Antholzner, who lived across the street from me when I was a young boy. "We went to the same church when we were younger," he said. It was discovered that we were both altar boys at this church, which was St. Magdalene located on the east side of Buffalo.

In another incident, I was on the rowing machine when I overheard two women talking about a trip to Ireland, and they mentioned a picture taken of a certain memorial. I said to them, "Was it by chance in a small town named Drimoleague?" To which they replied, "Yes, that's the name of the town." I answered with, "It's dedicated to my mother's brother, who was killed at the age of 24 in a civil war."

I happened to be on the treadmill when I engaged a young woman in a conversation. She told me that her name was Anya, and she had moved to America recently. She was from my father's home city of Kiev, in the Ukraine. I had a pleasant conversation about where my father was born. *(This was weird as I had now heard from both sides of my family.)*

I spoke with another man, who said to me, "You look familiar." After a few minutes of conversation we found out that we had been on the island of Kauai, in Hawaii, at the same time and passed each other on the walkway paths.

I want to mention that during my recovery period I decided to take lessons from professionals, in both golf and bowling, and have continued to enjoy both these sports.

When you read this article, it is my hope that you will look at life the way that I do, and enjoy your family first, and then notice the small things that people take for granted by stopping to "smell the roses," and enjoying life to the fullest.

Here it is 2007, and I am still here and enjoying good health. They have a new director here now. Her name is Jessica Nowak.[30] Sheila was promoted to another assignment.

Acknowledgment

I am dedicating this book to my dear wife Patricia, to my children, Jeanne, James, Bonnie, and Jennifer, and to my three stepchildren, Amy, Todd, and Christopher Proctor, as well as to my ex-partner and dear friend, Joe Schwartz.

And I want to give a special dedication to the policemen, firemen, rescue workers, and others who lost their lives on September 11, 2001, as well as the brave men and women of Flight 93, who gave their lives so that others may live when they crashed into a field in Shanksville, Pennsylvania.

Also an appreciation to Rudolph W. Giuliani, former mayor of New York City, who answered a letter I wrote about the declining crime around Times Square when my wife and I visited there. I was grateful to receive a personal reply on May 14, 2003.

A special recognition to former president William Jefferson Clinton, who was kind enough to reply to a letter which I wrote to him concerning my own heart attack, during the time period in which he was going through his. I was grateful to receive a personal reply on March 4, 2005.

Sincerely, Mickey Chernetsky
Detective Sergeant (Retired)

About the Author

Michael Chernetsky is a retired detective sergeant from the Buffalo Police Department. He lives in Kenmore, New York, with his wife Patricia and children.

The author served 34 years on the police department and received many letters of commendation including some from the FBI. He worked for 20 years on the robbery squad covering more than 100 bank robberies as well as other armed robberies.

The author saved the life of a gunshot victim when he was off duty and received an award from the mayor of the city of Buffalo, New York.

While working for the department he managed to receive a four-year degree in philosophy from the State University at New York.

In addition to surviving 34 years on a major police department, he survived a heart attack, heart surgery and a stroke.

Endnotes

[1] He became my first child's godfather (Jeanne).

[2] He had the cigar in his mouth when his retirement picture was in the paper.

[3] This officer died of cancer some years later.

[4] Of course, it was later determined that he was right about this, and it is a shame that they stalled on payment to the families of the guards who were killed, and just recently settled (2004), when they settled with the prisoners' families years before this.

[5] Years later Buffalo Police were ordered to take up the slack serving these warrants.

[6] *Exploring Philosophy* by Peter A Finch, pg 3-5, and Publishers Schenkman.

[7] A well-known killer and they sent him with only one guard!

[8] *An observation: anything that can go wrong will go wrong!*

+ *Years later I worked with a detective who was the son of this wrestler.*

[9] *This was the woman's phone number I had obtained from the bartender.*

[10] This particular precinct had the highest murder rate in the city.

[11] He killed couples in New York City.

[12] I am sorry to be writing this, but my friend Don Horn died of cancer some years later.

[13] This gangster died October 21, 2005, and they made a hero out of him when writing his obituary.

[14] I had worked with Tony on other occasions. He was an extra in the movie *Hide in Plain Sight*, and he also guarded James Caan and Robert Redford. He also made detective sergeant and retired from the homicide squad.

[15] John was shot in the line of duty several years later, and had to retire and walks with a limp.

[16] He used to practice judo with me. Most recently he had an article written in *The Buffalo News* dated May 8, 2007, about his heroics and the fact that he now has Parkinson's.

[17] This case ended up on *Nightline, with Ted Koppel,* who interviewed the arresting officer. Ted Koppel retired from anchoring *Nightline* November 22, 2005.

[18] *The Buffalo News*, May 6, 2005, stated that "FBI sources indicated that they will scale back its involvement in bank robbery investigations."

[19] This one detective died of cancer about a year later.

[20] This newspaper is now nonexistent.

[21] Chief Degenhart later became commissioner of police for the city of Buffalo, New York.

[22] I only used his initial to protect his identity

[23] This warrant was two years old and he and a companion tried to attack me while I worked a second job.

[24] He was killed by prisoners during the Attica prison riot.

[25] His wife sat up in bed and said the rosary for him at that time!

[26] An observation: anything that can go wrong will go wrong!

[27] This warrant was two years old and he and a companion tried to attack me while I was working a second job in a supermarket.

[28] Sheila Csiceri later became facility director.

[29] I am sorry to be writing this but Ralph died at the end of 2004.

[30] Jessica Nowak was recognized as the New York State Recreation & Parks Society's Young Professional of the year.